# Deconstructing the DUI

A Brief Guide to DUI Law in South Carolina

*First Edition*

By

Daniel M. Coble, Esq.

Everyday Evidence
Books by Daniel M. Coble

I would like to thank all of the defense attorneys, prosecutors, and judges who have helped me better understand the DUI laws in South Carolina.

# Table of Authorities

## Cases

City of Columbia v. Moore ................................................36

City of Rock Hill v. Suchenski ...................................... 16, 42

State v. Allen ................................................................. 6

State v. Dantonio ...........................................................43

State v. Douglas ............................................................43

State v. Elwell..............................................................39

State v. Gilliam .............................................................4

State v. Gordon............................................................27, 28

State v. Groome ......................................................... 13, 14

State v. Henkel .........................................................23, 29

State v. Hercheck........................................................40

State v. Huntley...........................................................38

State v. Jansen ............................................................40

State v. Kerr ............................................................... 7, 8

State v. Kimbrell..........................................................37

State v. Landis..........................................................17, 18

State v. McKnight.........................................................11

State v. Medley.........................................................30, 31

State v. Mimms........................................................ 11, 12

State v. Moore ............................................................11

State v. Parker .........................................................40, 41

State v. Pradubsri..........................................................9

State v. Provet.............................................................10

State v. Russell .............................................................2

State v. Salisbury ..........................................................7

State v. Taylor .....................................................17, 26, 27

State v. Townsend ................................................ 1, 2, 3, 4

State v. Williams .................................................................................14
Teamer v. State.................................................................... 19, 22, 24
Town of Mt. Pleasant v. Roberts ..................................................... 17, 25

## Statutes

S.C. Code Ann. § 56-5-130 ....................................................................5

S.C. Code Ann. § 56-5-165 ....................................................................5

S.C. Code Ann. § 56-5-2930 ..................................................................1

S.C. Code Ann. § 56-5-2950 ...........................................................32, 36

S.C. Code Ann. § 56-5-2953 (A) (1) ...............................................15, 30

S.C. Code Ann. § 56-5-2953 (A) (2) ....................................................38

S.C. Code Ann. § 56-5-2953 (B) ....................................................17, 21

## DUI Statute Reference

S.C. Code Ann.

**2930**: DUI offense and penalties and ADSAP

**2933**: DUAC offense and penalties and ADSAP

**2941**: Ignition interlock device

**2945**: Felony DUI

**2950(A)**: Implied consent: procedure for administering chemical test

**2950(B)**: Implied consent: before administering test, must advise (verbally and written and video record) defendant of certain rights

**2951**: License suspension for refusal/certain level

**2953(A)(1)**: Incident site recording requirements

**2953(A)(2)**: Breath site recording requirements

**2953(B)**: Exceptions to not recording

**2990**: Suspension of license after conviction

# Table of Contents

Driving Under the Influence ............................................................ 1

    *Driving* ...................................................................... 3

    *A motor vehicle* ........................................................... 4

    *In this state* ................................................................. 6

    *While under the influence* ............................................. 6

    *Materially and appreciably impaired* ........................... 7

The Stop ....................................................................................... 9

    *Reasonable suspicion* ................................................. 9

    *Observations of impaired driving* .............................. 11

    *Checkpoints* ............................................................... 12

Incident Site................................................................................15

    *Requirements of Recording* ....................................... 15

    *Arresting officer must tape*........................................ 17

    *No Video/Affidavit* .................................................... 19

    *Collision/wreck (Teamer)* .......................................... 22

    *Car not equipped with camera?* ................................ 25

    *Need to video majority of encounter* ........................ 26

    *Video of HGN (Gordon)* .............................................. 27

    *Field Sobriety Tests* ................................................... 28

    *Re-administer FST (Henkel)* ....................................... 29

    *Miranda* ................................................................... 30

Breath Test .................................................................................32

    *Implied Consent* ........................................................ 32

*Breath test offered first* ............................................................ 36

*Timing of breath test* ............................................................... 37

*Problem with machine*.............................................................. 38

*Requirements of Recording* ..................................................... 38

*Introduction of Results into Evidence* ..................................... 40

*Noncompliance: 2953 vs. 2950*................................................. 41

**Directed Verdict**.........................................................................**43**

*Standard* .................................................................................... 43

*Probable Cause for Arrest*........................................................ 43

**Penalties** ......................................................................................**44**

*DUI 1st* ........................................................................................ 44

*DUI 2nd* ....................................................................................... 44

*DUI 3rd*......................................................................................... 45

*DUI 4th or Subsequent* .............................................................. 45

**Case Law** .....................................................................................**46**

*Teamer* ...................................................................................... 46

*Henkel*........................................................................................ 59

*Suchenski* .................................................................................. 67

*Gordon*....................................................................................... 73

*Taylor*......................................................................................... 80

**SLED Regulations**.......................................................................**91**

**Statute** .......................................................................................**134**

# **Preface**

Prosecuting and defending DUI cases can be extremely difficult. There are many statutes and cases in this area of law. This book is only meant to be a guide book in exploring the basic concepts of the law.

A DUI is divided into certain stages. Some stages have statutory requirements that must be met, while other stages are gray areas. Let's deconstruct the typical DUI and see each stage.

# Driving Under the Influence

Before we get too far into the weeds, let's take a look at the Corpus Delicti of DUI: [1]

1. Driving
2. A motor vehicle
3. In this state
4. While under the influence of alcohol/drugs
5. Faculties to drive are materially and appreciably impaired

## Case Law

"While evidence of the *corpus delicti* in a particular case must be established by the best proof attainable, direct evidence is not essential. The *corpus delicti* may be sufficiently proved by presumptive or circumstantial evidence when that is the best obtainable." State v. Townsend, 321 S.C. 55, 57 (Ct. App. 1996) (citation omitted)

"The act of operating a motor vehicle with impaired faculties is the gravamen of the offense. The *corpus delicti* of DUI is: (1) driving a vehicle; (2) within this State; (3) while under the

---

[1] S.C. Code Ann. § 56-5-2930.

influence of intoxicating liquors, drugs, or any other substance of like character." State v. Townsend, 321 S.C. 55, 58 (Ct. App. 1996) (citation omitted)


"Finally, we conclude the evidence presented by the State was sufficient to establish the *corpus delicti* of the crime, if believed. The *corpus delicti* of DUI based upon alcohol is: (1) driving a motor vehicle; (2) within this state; (3) while under the influence of alcohol to the extent that the person's faculties to drive are materially and appreciably impaired. Russell admits that he was highly intoxicated from the time of the party through his arrest, such that his faculties were materially and appreciably impaired. We have already determined there was substantial independent evidence corroborating the fact that he was driving the car. The position and condition of the vehicle provides substantial circumstantial evidence that it was being operated in South Carolina. Therefore, the *corpus delicti* of the crime has been established." State v. Russell, 345 S.C. 128, 134 (Ct. App. 2001) (citations omitted)

2

# _Driving_

The State has to prove that the defendant actually drove the vehicle.[2]   This is more straightforward in a traffic stop or checkpoint.   But what about when a collision happens and the defendant has left the vehicle before law enforcement arrives?

Circumstantial evidence may be used to show that the defendant had driven the vehicle.[3]

## Case Law

"In the case before us, the state relied on the following circumstances to prove its case. Townsend was at the scene where his car had been involved in a wreck. He smelled like alcohol, failed field sobriety tests, and appeared to be intoxicated. A breathalyzer test showed his blood alcohol level to be .21. This is enough evidence, albeit circumstantial evidence, to submit the case to the jury. _Brown v. State,_ 307 S.C. 465 (1992) (a case should be submitted to the jury if there is any substantial evidence, either direct or circumstantial, which tends to prove the guilt of the accused or from which his guilt may be fairly and logically deduced); _State v. White,_ 311 S.C. 289 (Ct.App.1993)

---

[2] Id.

[3] State v. Townsend, 321 S.C. 55, 58 (Ct. App. 1996).

(precise questions of whether defendant drove motor vehicle while under the influence of alcohol or drugs were properly left to the jury as factfinders)." State v. Townsend, 321 S.C. 55, 58 (Ct. App. 1996)

"Uncontradicted evidence was presented that the respondent was found alone on the passenger side of a wrecked automobile, which had gone down an embankment on the right hand side of the highway. The operator of a tow truck arrived at the scene about fifteen (15) minutes after the accident occurred. He testified that the respondent smelled of alcohol and appeared to be under the influence. There was also testimony that respondent was 'rambling' in his conversation, when interviewed at the hospital a short time later, 'just talking out of his head;' but admitted that he was driving his automobile at the time of the accident. An open bottle of an alcoholic beverage was found in the automobile.

The foregoing evidence amply supports the submission of the case to the jury." State v. Gilliam, 270 S.C. 345, 347, 242 S.E.2d 410, 411 (1978)

## _A motor vehicle_

**SECTION 56-5-130**. Motor vehicle defined.

Every vehicle which is self-propelled, except mopeds, and every vehicle which is propelled by electric power obtained from overhead trolley wires, but not operated upon rails, is a "motor vehicle".[4]

**SECTION 56-5-165**. Moped defined.

Notwithstanding the provisions of Section 56-5-160, every cycle with pedals to permit propulsion by human power or without pedals and with a motor of not more than fifty cubic centimeters which produces not to exceed two brake horsepower and which is not capable of propelling the vehicle at a speed in excess of thirty miles an hour on level ground is a moped. If an internal combustion engine is used, the moped must have a power drive system that functions directly or automatically without clutching or shifting by the operator after the drive system is engaged.[5]

---

[4] S.C. Code Ann. § 56-5-130.
[5] S.C. Code Ann. § 56-5-165.

# _In this state_

The statute makes it against the law to commit DUI anywhere within this state.[6] This includes private property.[7]

## Case Law

"To construe § 56-5-6310 as appellant suggests would leave our DUI law applicable to all property within the State, public or private, with the particular exception of private _roads_. Under this reasoning, a DUI offense committed on a property owner's driveway could not be prosecuted absent the owner's previous written consent but an offense committed on the abutting private property could. The legislature could not have intended such an exception to application of our DUI law." State v. Allen, 314 S.C. 539, 541–42 (1993)

# _While under the influence_

The State must prove that the defendant was impaired by either alcohol, drugs, or a combination of both.[8]

## Case Law

---

[6] S.C. Code Ann. § 56-5-2930.

[7] State v. Allen, 314 S.C. 539, 541–42 (1993).

[8] S.C. Code Ann. § 56-5-2930.

"In the instant case, there was sufficient direct evidence establishing the elements of DUI and the identity of the perpetrator, such that the circumstantial evidence was merely corroborative. In South Carolina, the corpus delicti of DUI must be established by proof that a person's ability to drive has been materially and appreciably impaired by the use of alcohol and/or drugs. In other words, the State has to prove: (1) Salisbury's ability to drive was materially and appreciably impaired; and (2) this impairment was caused by the use of drugs or alcohol." State v. Salisbury, 343 S.C. 520, 524 (2001) (citations omitted)

# *Materially and appreciably impaired*

On one hand, a defendant does not have to be drunk in order to have his faculties materially and appreciably impaired.[9]

On the other hand, having consumed alcohol or drugs does not automatically mean that the defendant's faculties are materially and appreciably impaired.[10]

## Case Law

---

[9] State v. Kerr, 330 S.C. 132, 144 (Ct. App. 1998).
[10] Id.

"The trial judge properly charged the jury in part on the standard of proof necessary to establish driving under the influence. However, he improperly instructed the jury to use the standard of one's driving 'who had not drunk any intoxicating beverage.' Prior case law speaks in terms of the ability to operate a vehicle with reasonable care and as a prudent driver with due regard for himself and others. These are proper standards with which to compare the defendant when determining whether defendant's driving abilities were materially and appreciably impaired. The trial judge also instructed the jury to consider the standard of a driver who had not partaken of any intoxicating beverage. One violates the statute by operating a motor vehicle where he has partaken an intoxicating beverage to the extent that he cannot drive a motor vehicle with reasonable care, or cannot drive as a prudent driver would operate a vehicle." State v. Kerr, 330 S.C. 132, 144 (Ct. App. 1998)

# The Stop

A faulty stop does not automatically lead to dismissal. Rather, it can lead to excluding everything that happened from the stop. This may be considered a distinction without a difference.

## *Reasonable suspicion*

In order for an officer to pull someone over, he must have reasonable suspicion that a crime has occurred. This standard is lower than probable cause.[11]

Many DUIs begin with a traffic stop, so the first question will be whether or not the officer had reasonable suspicion to pull them over.

### Case Law

"Reasonable suspicion is more than a general hunch but less than what is required for probable cause" State v. Pradubsri, 420 S.C. 629

"Violation of motor vehicle codes provides an officer reasonable suspicion to initiate a traffic stop. A traffic stop supported by reasonable suspicion of a traffic violation remains valid until the

---

[11] State v. Pradubsri, 420 S.C. 629.

purpose of the traffic stop has been completed. The officer may not extend the duration of a traffic stop in order to question the motorist on unrelated matters unless he possesses reasonable suspicion that warrants an additional seizure of the motorist. The officer cannot avoid this rule by employing dilatory tactics. See United States v. Jones, 234 F.2d 234 (5th Cir. 2000) (driver's Fourth Amendment rights violated when, after dispatcher reported no problems and officer had completed warning citation except for obtaining the driver's signature, officer deliberately delayed completing the stop for several more minutes until canine search unit arrived)." State v. Provet, 405 S.C. 101, 108 (2013) (citations omitted)


"'Violation of motor vehicle codes provides an officer reasonable suspicion to initiate a traffic stop...The test whether reasonable suspicion exists is an objective assessment of the circumstances; the officer's subjective motivations are irrelevant.' '[C]ourts must give due weight to common sense judgments reached by officers in light of their experience and training.' At bottom, in evaluating whether an officer possesses reasonable suspicion, this Court must 'consider the totality of the circumstances—the whole picture'" State v. Moore, 415 S.C. 245, 252–53 (2016)

"A pre-trial order granting the suppression of evidence which significantly impairs the prosecution of a criminal case is directly appealable under S.C. Code Ann. § 14–3–330(2)(a) (1976)." State v. McKnight, 287 S.C. 167, 168 (1985)

## *Observations of impaired driving*

An officer's observation of the vehicle can also be used to determine if there is reasonable suspicion to make the traffic stop.[12]

### Case Law

"Mimms correctly asserts the pertinent statute 'does not penalize the act of leaving a lane of travel on one occasion' and that fact alone does not render her driving impaired. However, during oral argument before this court, Mimms conceded Trooper Burris had probable cause to initiate the stop. In fact, Mimms never argued to the magistrate court or circuit court Trooper Burris did not have

---

[12] State v. Mimms, No. 2014-UP-489, 2014 WL 7898503, at *6 (S.C. Ct. App. July 30, 2014).

probable cause to make the stop. The State produced a great deal of evidence of impaired driving uncovered after the initial stop. Specifically, the State submitted evidence: (1) Mimms' car matched the description of a car driving erratically; (2) while responding to the dispatch, Burris observed Mimms run off the roadway; (3) during the stop, Burris told Mimms 'You [were] weaving all over the roadway'; (4) Burris 'smelled an odor of alcohol' as he walked toward Mimms' car and inside her vehicle; (5) Mimms did not successfully complete the HGN test; (6) during the HGN test, Mimms was unable to keep her balance; (7) based on Mimms' performance on the HGN test, Burris 'did not feel comfortable' requiring Mimms to complete additional field sobriety tests; and (8) Mimms' appearance and mannerisms indicated she was under the influence of alcohol. Therefore, viewing the evidence in the light most favorable to the State, the evidence supports the magistrate's submission of this case to the jury." State v. Mimms, No. 2014-UP-489, 2014 WL 7898503, at *6 (S.C. Ct. App. July 30, 2014)

## *Checkpoints*

Checkpoints are a very common situation where DUIs take place. The United States Supreme Court has held that law enforcement cannot set up checkpoints for general crime deterrent. Rather, they have to have a specific reason as well as several other criteria.[13]

The judge will conduct a hearing to determine if the checkpoint meets the constitutional requirements.[14] However, remember, that if the defendant did not actually go through the checkpoint, then no such hearing is required.[15]

## Case Law

"In *Edmond,* the Court held that a police checkpoint whose primary purpose is general crime control- in Edmond narcotics interdiction- is unreasonable under the Fourth Amendment." State v. Groome, 378 S.C. 615, 618 (2008)

"The circuit court went on to find that even if the primary purpose were a license checkpoint and thus the roadblock passed constitutional muster under *Edmond,* the roadblock would still violate the Fourth Amendment under *Brown v. Texas,* 443 U.S.

---

[13] City of Indianapolis v. Edmond, 531 U.S. 32 (2000).
[14] State v. Williams, 417 S.C. 209, 220 (Ct. App. 2016).
[15] Id.

47 (1979). *Brown* established a three part balancing test for determining the constitutionality of a traffic checkpoint:

1) the gravity of the public interest served by the seizure;

2) the degree to which the seizure serves the public interest; and,

3) the severity of the interference with individual liberty."

State v. Groome. at 619

"In the present case, the magistrate erred in finding the State had to establish the constitutionality of the checkpoint. Both *Scheetz*, 293 F.3d at 183, and *Griffin*, 749 S.E.2d at 447, hold the analysis for determining if a checkpoint is constitutional only applies when a vehicle is stopped at the checkpoint and does not apply when the vehicle does not actually make it to the checkpoint. Here, Williams turned around before he got to the checkpoint; thus, he was never actually stopped by the checkpoint. Accordingly, the magistrate erred in requiring the State to prove the checkpoint was constitutional." State v. Williams, 417 S.C. 209, 220 (Ct. App. 2016)

# Incident Site

The statute and case law are clear that an officer must video record at the incident location of the DUI.[16] The video has several requirements that must be recorded, and the video has to be recorded by the arresting officer.[17] If the officer did not record, then an exception must apply to avoid dismissal.[18]

A common issue that arises with DUI cases is when the arresting officer did record the incident site, however, there is some problem with the video (e.g., no audio, defendant stepped out of video, etc.).

## *Requirements of Recording*

The incident site recording must: [19]

1. not begin later than the activation of the officer's blue lights;
2. include any field sobriety tests administered; and
3. include the arrest of a person for a violation of Section 56-5-2930 or Section 56-5-2933, or a probable cause

---

[16] S.C. Code Ann. § 56-5-2953.
[17] S.C. Code Ann. § 56-5-2953 (A) (1).
[18] S.C. Code Ann. § 56-5-2953 (B).
[19] S.C. Code Ann. § 56-5-2953 (A) (1).

determination in that the person violated Section 56-5-2945, and show the person being advised of his Miranda rights.

The S.C. Supreme Court in *Suchenski* held that if there is a violation of the video recording requirement and no exceptions apply then the DUI may be dismissed.[20]

## Case Law

"Under § 56-5-2953, a violation of the statute, with no mention of prejudice, may result in dismissal of the charges. The statute provides, 'Failure by the arresting officer to produce the videotapes required by this section **is not alone a ground for dismissal** of any charge made pursuant to Section 56-5-2930, 56-5-2933, or 56-5-2945 **if** [exceptions apply] ...' (emphasis added). Conversely, failure to produce videotapes would be a ground for dismissal if no exceptions apply...Finally, dismissal of the DUAC charge is an appropriate remedy provided by § 56-5-2953 where a violation of subsection (A) is not mitigated by subsection (B) exceptions." City of Rock Hill v. Suchenski, 374 S.C. 12, 16-17 (2007).

---

[20] City of Rock Hill v. Suchenski, 374 S.C. 12, 16-17 (2007).

"A violation of this section may result in dismissal of the DUI charges. S.C. Code Ann. § 56–5–2953(B) (Supp.2013); *see also City of Rock Hill v. Suchenski,* 374 S.C. 12, 17, 646 S.E.2d 879, 881 (2007) (holding dismissal of DUI charge is an appropriate remedy if the officer fails to produce a **satisfactory** video recording unless an exception applies)." State v. Taylor, 411 S.C. 294, 301 (Ct. App. 2014) (emphasis added)

"By requiring a law enforcement agency to videotape a DUI arrest, the Legislature clearly intended strict compliance with the provisions of section 56–5–2953 and, in turn, promulgated a severe sanction for noncompliance." Town of Mt. Pleasant v. Roberts, 393 S.C. 332, 349 (2011)

## *Arresting officer must tape*

The statute requires that the "arresting officer" video record the incident site.[21] What if there are multiple officers responding to the scene? How do you determine who the arresting officer is? The case *Landis* helps define who the arresting officer is.[22]

---

[21] S.C. Code Ann. § 56-5-2953 (B).
[22] State v. Landis, 362 S.C. 97, 104 (Ct. App. 2004).

# Case Law

"Pellucidly, the record supports the finding that Trooper Davis was the 'arresting officer' as that phrase is ordinarily understood. Trooper Davis personally observed Landis' driving prior to the traffic stop. He arrived at the scene simultaneously with the State Transport Officer. Trooper Davis pulled in directly behind the Transport Officer and approached just after Landis had been removed from his vehicle. Moreover, Trooper Davis conducted the field sobriety test, determined Landis was impaired, and **placed him under arrest** for DUI...Trooper Davis 'restrained [Landis] of his liberty' and brought him 'within the custody and control of the law.' Therefore, we hold that the State Transport Officer merely assisted in facilitating the traffic stop. Trooper Davis was the arresting officer responsible for meeting the statutory videotaping requirements of section 56–5–2953(A)." State v. Landis, 362 S.C. 97, 104 (Ct. App. 2004).

# _No Video/Affidavit_

There are four exceptions to the requirement that the officer record in the incident site. Two of them require the officer to fill out an affidavit: [23]

1. if the arresting officer submits a sworn affidavit certifying the video equipment was inoperable despite efforts to maintain it

2. if the arresting officer submits a sworn affidavit that it was impossible to produce the videotape because the defendant either (a) needed emergency medical treatment or (b) exigent circumstances existed;

3. in circumstances including, but not limited to, road blocks, traffic accidents, and citizens' arrests; or

4. for any other valid reason for the failure to produce the videotape based upon the totality of the circumstances.

---

**SECTION 56-5-2953.** Incident site and breath test site video recording.

---

[23] Teamer v. State, 416 S.C. 171, 177 (2016).

19

**(B)** Nothing in this section may be construed as prohibiting the introduction of other relevant evidence in the trial of a violation of Section 56-5-2930, 56-5-2933, or 56-5-2945. Failure by the arresting officer to produce the video recording required by this section is not alone a ground for dismissal of any charge made pursuant to Section 56-5-2930, 56-5-2933, or 56-5-2945 if the arresting officer submits a sworn affidavit certifying that the video recording equipment at the time of the arrest or probable cause determination, or video equipment at the breath test facility was in an inoperable condition, stating which reasonable efforts have been made to maintain the equipment in an operable condition, and certifying that there was no other operable breath test facility available in the county or, in the alternative, submits a sworn affidavit certifying that it was physically impossible to produce the video recording because the person needed emergency medical treatment, or exigent circumstances existed. In circumstances including, but not limited to, road blocks, traffic accident investigations, and citizens' arrests, where an arrest has been made and the video recording equipment has not been activated by blue lights, the failure by the arresting officer to produce the video recordings required by this section is not alone a ground for dismissal. However, as soon as video recording is practicable in these circumstances, video recording must begin and conform with the provisions of this section. Nothing in this section prohibits the court from considering any other valid reason for the failure to produce the video recording based upon the totality of the circumstances; nor do the provisions of this section prohibit the person from offering evidence relating to the arresting law enforcement officer's failure to produce the video recording.[24]

## Case Law

"We have previously interpreted the exceptions in subsection (B) to not require a sworn affidavit in all circumstances:

'Subsection (B) of section 56–5–2953 outlines several statutory exceptions that excuse noncompliance with the mandatory videotaping requirements. Noncompliance is excusable[ ](1) if the arresting officer submits a sworn affidavit certifying the video equipment was inoperable despite efforts to maintain it; (2) if the arresting officer submits a sworn affidavit that it was impossible

---

[24] S.C. Code Ann. § 56-5-2953 (B).

to produce the videotape because the defendant either (a) needed emergency medical treatment or (b) exigent circumstances existed; (3) in circumstances including, but not limited to, road blocks, traffic accidents, and citizens' arrests; or (4) for any other valid reason for the failure to produce the videotape based upon the totality of the circumstances.'

Thus, based on this Court's interpretation of the statute in *Roberts,* an affidavit is not needed to qualify for the third and fourth exceptions. As Respondent was arrested for FSBL in connection with a traffic accident, this case falls within the third exception." Teamer v. State, 416 S.C. 171, 177 (2016) (citation omitted)

## *Collision/wreck (Teamer)*

What happens when the DUI case is not a typical traffic stop, but rather a collision case?

A judge may find that under the collision scenario, the officer is excused from the videotaping requirements under the accident exception.[25]

---

[25] Id.

However, this does not give the officer an unconditional excuse to not videotape. As held in *Henkel*, the officer must begin recording as soon as practicable.[26]

## Case Law

"Accordingly, we hold when an individual's conduct is videotaped during a situation provided for in subsection (B), compliance with subsection (A) must begin at the time videotaping becomes practicable and continue until the arrest is complete." State v. Henkel, 413 S.C. 9, 15–16 (2015)

"This Court has recently interpreted the third exception, regarding traffic accidents, to excuse the videotaping requirement only up to the point where videotaping becomes practicable. *State v. Henkel,* 413 S.C. 9, 14 (2015). Here, because Respondent's vehicle's headlights were off, Deputy Evett could not see Respondent's vehicle until it collided with the other vehicle. Once the accident occurred, the urgency of the situation (calling for back-up, assessing injuries, and securing Respondent who was attempting to flee) understandably became Deputy Evett's primary concerns. We further note Respondent was not suspected

---

[26] State v. Henkel, 413 S.C. 9, 15–16 (2015).

of DUI until Corporal Darity spoke with Respondent at the hospital.

The failure to initiate videotaping in this case could also be excused under the totality of the circumstances, which is the fourth exception. As this Court recognized in *Henkel,* 'Subsection (A) was intended to capture the interactions and field sobriety testing between the subject and the officer in a typical DUI traffic stop where there are no other witnesses.' *Id.* This situation, created solely by Respondent's dangerous and evasive driving, does not resemble a typical traffic stop. As Respondent was pursued and arrested in connection with the FSBL charge and was not charged with felony DUI until after he was transported to the hospital, no field sobriety tests were administered or could have been captured on video. The legislative concerns with videotaping one-on-one traffic stops are not implicated under the facts of this case, and under the totality of the circumstances, Deputy Evett's failure to produce a videotape was reasonable and excusable." Teamer v. State, 416 S.C. 171, 178 (2016)

# _Car not equipped with camera?_

Most law enforcement agencies in this state are equipped with cameras in their vehicles. However, if the officer's vehicle is not equipped with a camera, then they will need an affidavit explaining the reason why.[27]

## Case Law

"Taking into consideration the purpose of section 56–5–2953, which is to create direct evidence of a DUI arrest, we find the Town's protracted failure to equip its patrol vehicles with video cameras, despite its 'priority' ranking, defeats the intent of the Legislature and violates the statutorily-created obligation to videotape DUI arrests. Accordingly, we do not believe that the Town should be able to continually evade its duty by relying on subsection (G) of section 56–5–2953. Thus, we hold that the Town's failure to equip its patrol vehicles does not negate the application of the statutory exceptions in subsection (B)." Town of Mt. Pleasant v. Roberts, 393 S.C. 332, 347 (2011)

---

[27] Town of Mt. Pleasant v. Roberts, 393 S.C. 332, 347 (2011).

# _Need to video majority of encounter_

While the statute is clear that the officer must record the incident site, the Supreme Court has stated that the video must record the majority of the requirements.[28]

## Case Law

"The plain language of the statute demonstrates the legislature intended video recording of the majority of an officer's encounter with a potential DUI suspect. Nonetheless, interpreting the statute to require dismissal of the charges when the defendant is off camera for a short period of time and the gap does not occur during any of those events that either create direct evidence of a DUI or serve important rights of the defendant would result in an absurdity that could not possibly have been intended by the legislature. Indeed, interpreting the statute in that way would require dismissal of a DUI charge when a suspect stumbles out of view of the camera or when the officer is placing a suspect into his vehicle. Accordingly, section 56–5–2953 does not require dismissal of a DUI charge when the video recording of the incident briefly omits the suspect but that omission does not occur during any of those events that either create direct evidence of a

---

[28] State v. Taylor, 411 S.C. 294, 306 (Ct. App. 2014).

DUI or serve important rights of the defendant." State v. Taylor, 411 S.C. 294, 306 (Ct. App. 2014)

# *Video of HGN (Gordon)*

A common field sobriety test used in DUI cases is the horizontal gaze nystagmus test (HGN). What happens when the officer records the test, but for some reason parts of the test are problematic and not viewable? Follow the common sense test put out by *Gordon*.[29]

## Case Law

"Accordingly, the circuit court's finding that the head must be visible does not amount to a hyper-technicality, but merely states the obvious. The Court of Appeals did not err in affirming this requirement.

Here, the officer's administration of the HGN test is visible on the video recording. It is undisputed that Gordon's face is depicted in the video; it is axiomatic that the face is a part of the head. The officer's flashlight and arm are visible as he administers the test. Also, the officer's instructions were audible. Thus, the requirement that the head be visible on the video is met and the

---

[29] State v. Gordon, 414 S.C. 94, 99–100 (2015).

statutory requirement that the administration of the HGN field sobriety test be video recorded is satisfied. Therefore, the per se dismissal of the charge as discussed in *Town of Mount Pleasant v. Roberts* and *City of Rock Hill v. Suchenski* is not appropriate. Even if we assume that the video of a field sobriety test is of such poor quality that its admission is more prejudicial than probative, the remedy would not be to dismiss the DUI charge. Instead, the remedy would be to redact the field sobriety test from the video and exclude testimony about the test. If that remedy is applied here, there is still sufficient evidence to present this case to a jury for resolution. The evidence included the breath alcohol analysis report, video of other field sobriety tests, and Gordon's statement that he had consumed four beers." State v. Gordon, 414 S.C. 94, 99–100 (2015)

## *Field Sobriety Tests*

It appears that the Supreme Court in *Gordon* created a common sense requirement for recording field sobriety tests.

- First and foremost, was there a recording of the FST?
- Second, did the recording capture the part of the FST, using common sense, that is needed to show that the officer properly administered the FST?

28

- Third, if the common sense portion was captured, then any poor quality of the tape should be excluded or admitted based on Rule 403. Suppression of the evidence, not dismissal of the case is proper.

# *Re-administer FST (Henkel)*

What happens when an officer does not record one of the requirements under 2953 (A), but he falls under a valid exception to the requirement under (B)? Does he have to re-administer the FST or Miranda? In *Henkel*, the Supreme Court said that he does not have to re-administer.[30]

## Case Law

"Requiring an officer to repeat *Miranda* and field sobriety tests on camera in a situation contemplated in subsection (B) is not consistent with the legislative intent of the DUI recording statute." State v. Henkel, 413 S.C. 9, 15 (2015)

---

[30] Henkel, 413 S.C. 9, 15 (2015).

# _Miranda_

The video recording of the incident site must show the defendant being advised of his Miranda rights.[31]  But also remember, even if the State has complied with the statute, there can still be a constitutional issue with the Miranda warnings that could result in suppression of any statements.[32]

**Case Law**

"As our supreme court noted, '[i]n _Seibert_, the [U.S. Supreme] Court dealt with the police practice of questioning a suspect until 'incriminating       information       is       elicited,       then administering _Miranda_ warnings. Following the warnings, the suspect is again questioned and the incriminating information re-elicited. The post-warning statement is then sought to be admitted.' _Navy_, 386 S.C. at 302. To determine whether a constitutional violation occurred in this setting, a court must analyze the following factors: (1) 'the completeness and detail of the question and answers in the first round of interrogation,' (2) 'the timing and setting of the first questioning and the second,'

---

[31] S.C. Code Ann. § 56-5-2953 (A) (1).
[32] <u>State v. Medley</u>, 417 S.C. 18, 27–28 (Ct. App. 2016).

(3) 'the continuity of police personnel,' and (4) 'the degree to which the interrogator's questions treated the second round as continuous with the first." State v. Medley, 417 S.C. 18, 27–28 (Ct. App. 2016)

# Breath Test

Simply put: under South Carolina law, a person who drives in this state gives implied consent to be tested for alcohol or drugs if they are arrested for driving under the influence.[33]

If a person is arrested for DUI and the officer wants a test to be done, then there are certain procedures that the officer must follow under 56-5-2950 and 56-5-2953.

## *Implied Consent*

The implied consent law lays out specific requirements that must be met for a valid breath test procedure.[34]

Before any test may be administered, the defendant has to be verbally informed, as well as given a written copy, of his rights. This also must be video recorded.[35]

**SECTION 56-5-2950**. Implied consent to testing for alcohol or drugs; procedures; inference of DUI.

**(A)** A person who drives a motor vehicle in this State is

---

[33] S.C. Code Ann. § 56-5-2950.
[34] Id.
[35] Id.

considered to have given consent to chemical tests of the person's breath, blood, or urine for the purpose of determining the presence of alcohol, drugs, or the combination of alcohol and drugs, if arrested for an offense arising out of acts alleged to have been committed while the person was driving a motor vehicle while under the influence of alcohol, drugs, or a combination of alcohol and drugs. A breath test must be administered at the direction of a law enforcement officer who has arrested a person for driving a motor vehicle in this State while under the influence of alcohol, drugs, or a combination of alcohol and drugs. At the direction of the arresting officer, the person first must be offered a breath test to determine the person's alcohol concentration. If the person is physically unable to provide an acceptable breath sample because the person has an injured mouth, is unconscious or dead, or for any other reason considered acceptable by the licensed medical personnel, the arresting officer may request a blood sample to be taken. If the officer has reasonable suspicion that the person is under the influence of drugs other than alcohol, or is under the influence of a combination of alcohol and drugs, the officer may order that a urine sample be taken for testing. A breath sample taken for testing must be collected within two hours of the arrest. Any additional tests to collect other samples must be collected within three hours of the arrest. The breath test must be administered by a person trained and certified by the South Carolina Criminal Justice Academy, pursuant to SLED policies. Before the breath test is administered, an eight one-hundredths of one percent simulator test must be performed and the result must reflect a reading between 0.076 percent and 0.084 percent. Blood and urine samples must be obtained by physicians licensed by the State Board of Medical Examiners, registered nurses licensed by the State Board of Nursing, and other medical personnel trained to obtain the samples in a licensed medical facility. Blood and urine samples must be obtained and handled in accordance with procedures approved by SLED.

**(B)** No tests may be administered or samples obtained unless, upon activation of the video recording equipment and prior to the commencement of the testing procedure, the person has been given a written copy of and verbally informed that:

(1) the person does not have to take the test or give the samples, but that the person's privilege to drive must be suspended or denied for at least six months with the option of ending the suspension if the person enrolls in the Ignition Interlock Device Program, if the person refuses to submit to the test, and that the

34

person's refusal may be used against the person in court;

(2) the person's privilege to drive must be suspended for at least one month with the option of ending the suspension if the person enrolls in the Ignition Interlock Device Program, if the person takes the test or gives the samples and has an alcohol concentration of fifteen one-hundredths of one percent or more;

(3) the person has the right to have a qualified person of the person's own choosing conduct additional independent tests at the person's expense;

(4) the person has the right to request a contested case hearing within thirty days of the issuance of the notice of suspension; and

(5) if the person does not request a contested case hearing or if the person's suspension is upheld at the contested case hearing, the person shall enroll in an Alcohol and Drug Safety Action Program.[36]

---

[36] Id.

# _Breath test offered first_

"If the person is physically unable to provide an acceptable breath sample because the person has an injured mouth, is unconscious or dead, or for any other reason considered acceptable by the licensed medical personnel, the arresting officer may request a blood sample to be taken."[37]

## Case Law

"In the case at bar, it is undisputed Moore did not have an injury to the mouth and was conscious at all times. Therefore, the City was required under § 56-5-2950 to present evidence Moore was physically unable to give an acceptable breath sample for a reason found acceptable by licensed medical personnel. Because the City did not do so, the municipal court erred in admitting the blood sample into evidence." City of Columbia v. Moore, 318 S.C. 292, 295 (Ct. App. 1995)

---

[37] S.C. Code Ann. § 56-5-2950 (A).

"We conclude the plain meaning of the statute requires the arresting officer to offer a breath test, absent a valid determination that the defendant is physically unable to give an acceptable breath sample. Where the evidence shows a person is dead, unconscious, or physically unable to provide an acceptable breath sample as determined by authorized medical personnel, no breath test need first be offered, and the blood test results are admissible. Where the evidence establishes that an accused is offered a breath test, but agrees to the officer's request for a blood test in lieu thereof, the result is likewise admissible. Where the evidence establishes the accused has an obvious injury to the mouth that the arresting officer reasonably believes will interfere with providing an acceptable breath sample, the officer may order a blood test to be taken. Whether or not the officer's belief is reasonable will, of course, depend upon the circumstances of each case." State v. Kimbrell, 326 S.C. 344, 348–49 (Ct. App. 1997)

## *Timing of breath test*

The breath sample must be taken within two hours of the arrest. Any other tests must be collected within three hours.[38]

---

[38] Id.

## Case Law

"In substance, the amendment eliminated the three-hour videotaping requirement of subsection 56–5–2953(A)(2)(a) and inserted into subsection 56–5–2950(A) a requirement that '[a] breath sample taken for testing must be collected within two hours of the arrest." Consequently, the Act repealed or amended the existing law by eliminating an existing requirement for law enforcement officials in establishing an arrestee's blood-alcohol content and, in its place, instituting a new and different requirement." State v. Hilton, 406 S.C. 580, 587 (Ct. App. 2013)

# *Problem with machine*

## Case Law

"Evidence the simulator test was not run in conformity with Act 434 goes to the weight, not the admissibility, of Huntley's breathalyzer results." State v. Huntley, 349 S.C. 1, 6 (2002)

# *Requirements of Recording*

The incident site recording must: [39]

---

[39] S.C. Code Ann. § 56-5-2953 (A) (2).

1.  include the entire breath test procedure, the person being informed that he is being video recorded, and that he has the right to refuse the test;
2.  include the person taking or refusing the breath test and the actions of the breath test operator while conducting the test; and
3.  also include the person's conduct during the required twenty-minute pre-test waiting period, unless the officer submits a sworn affidavit certifying that it was physically impossible to video record this waiting period.

## Case Law

"Therefore, Elwell argues that in the present case, where a complete videotape was not produced, the Court should uphold the dismissal of the charges due to the State's violation of the statute. We agree that the proper remedy in this case for failure to comply with the statutory requirements elucidated in section 56–5–2953 would be dismissal." State v. Elwell, 403 S.C. 606, 614 (2013)

*Refusal as Evidence*

"Hence, it is well established in this State that one who is arrested for DUI impliedly consents to a breathalyzer test, and that the revocation of that consent is constitutionally admissible as prosecutorial evidence at the trial pursuant to that arrest." State v. Jansen, 305 S.C. 320, 322 (1991)

*20 Minute Wait Period*

"Once an arrestee refuses the breath test, the evidence gathering portion is over. As a consequence, we agree with the State that once Hercheck refused the test and no breath test was administered, the statute did not require the arresting officer to continue to videotape the twenty-minute pre-test waiting period, and therefore, the videotape produced at trial complied with the statutory requirements. To require otherwise, would result in the officer having to undergo a useless and absurd act." State v. Hercheck, 403 S.C. 597, 604 (2013)

# ***Introduction of Results into Evidence***

Even if the officer complied with the implied consent statute as well as the breath test recording statute, he still has to lay a proper foundation to have the results admitted into evidence.[40]

## **Case Law**

---

[40] State v. Parker, 271 S.C. 159, 162–63 (1978).

"'The party offering the results of any of these chemical tests (for drunkenness) must first lay a foundation by producing expert witnesses who will explain the way in which the test is conducted, identify it as approved under the statute, and vouch for its correct administration in the particular case.'

The question we are called upon to determine is, 'What foundation should be laid for the introduction of the results of the breathalyzer test?' The requirements are not the same in all states. We recommend the reading of State v. Baker, 56 Wash.2d 846, 355 P.2d 806 (1960), and follow with approval the requirements set forth by the Supreme Court of the State of Washington. Prior to admitting such evidence, the State may be required to prove (1) that the machine was in proper working order at the time of the test; (2) that the correct chemicals had been used; (3) that the accused was not allowed to put anything in his mouth for 20 minutes prior to the test, and (4) that the test was administered by a qualified person in the proper manner." State v. Parker, 271 S.C. 159, 162–63 (1978)

## *Noncompliance: 2953 vs. 2950*

What happens when an officer does not comply with 2953 and/or 2950?

Based on *Suchenski*, it appears that failure to comply with 2953 may be dismissal, while failure to comply with 2950 does not have to be dismissal.[41]

## Case Law

"The statute at issue in *Huntley* was the implied consent statute which required a simulator test before administration of a breath test. That statute, S.C. Code Ann. § 56-5-2950 (2006), is silent as to the remedy for noncompliance, whereas the statute in this case provides for dismissal of charges when the statute is inexcusably violated." City of Rock Hill v. Suchenski, 374 S.C. 12, 16 (2007)

---

[41] City of Rock Hill v. Suchenski, 374 S.C. 12, 16 (2007).

# Directed Verdict

## *Standard*

"The criterion for denying a directed verdict motion in South Carolina is well established. A case should be submitted to the jury if there is any direct evidence or any substantial circumstantial evidence that reasonably tends to prove the guilt of the accused or from which guilt may be fairly and logically deduced."[42]

## *Probable Cause for Arrest*

"The testimony of the arresting officer shows that he observed the defendant operating his automobile from one side of the road to the other; and that at the time of arrest the defendant had a strong odor of alcohol about him, could not stand or walk without assistance, and his speech, both as to clarity and coherence, was affected. Under the foregoing testimony of the arresting officer, the exception charging error in the refusal of the trial court to direct a verdict of not guilty is totally without merit."[43]

---

[42] State v. Dantonio, 376 S.C. 594, 603 (Ct. App. 2008).
[43] State v. Douglas, 245 S.C. 83, 86 (1964).

# Penalties

## DUI 1st

| Under .10 |
| --- |
| • $400 Fine; or<br>• 48 hours – 30 days; or<br>• 48 hours public service |
| *.10 - .16*<br>• $500 Fine; or<br>• 72 hours – 30 days; or<br>• 72 hours public service |
| *Above .16*<br>• $1000 Fine; or<br>• 30 days – 90 days; or<br>• 30 days public service |

## DUI 2nd

| Under .10 |
| --- |
| • $1,100 – $5,100 Fine; and<br>• 5 days – 1 year; |
| *.10 - .16*<br>• $1,100 – $5,500 Fine; and<br>• 30 days – 2 years; |
| *Above .16*<br>• $1,100 – $6,500 Fine; and<br>• 90 days – 3 years; |

# _DUI 3rd_

| |
|---|
| _Under .10_<br>    •  $3,800 – $6,300 Fine; and<br>    •  60 days – 3 years; |
| _.10 - .16_<br>    •  $5,000 – $7,500 Fine; and<br>    •  90 days – 4 years; |
| _Above .16_<br>    •  $7,500 – $10,00 Fine; and<br>    •  6 months – 5 years; |

# _DUI 4th or Subsequent_

| |
|---|
| _Under .10_<br>    •  1 year – 5 years |
| _.10 - .16_<br>    •  2 years – 6 years |
| _Above .16_<br>    •  3 years – 7 years |

# Case Law

## *Teamer*

416 S.C. 171
Supreme Court of South Carolina.

Nathaniel TEAMER, Respondent,
v.
STATE of South Carolina, Petitioner.

**Opinion**

Justice KITTREDGE.

**\*173** This is a post-conviction relief (PCR) matter. Respondent Nathaniel Teamer was convicted of first-degree burglary, felony driving under the influence (DUI) resulting in great bodily injury, and failure to stop for a blue light (FSBL) resulting in great bodily injury and sentenced to an aggregate term of thirty years in prison. Following the court of appeals' dismissal of Respondent's direct appeal, Respondent filed a PCR application. The PCR court granted relief on four grounds. We granted the State's petition for a writ of certiorari to review the PCR court's decision. We reverse and reinstate Respondent's convictions and sentences.

**\*174 I.**

The State first argues the PCR court erred in finding Respondent's trial counsel ineffective for failing to move for dismissal of Respondent's

DUI charge. Specifically, the State argues the PCR court erred in determining the motion to dismiss likely would have been successful because the PCR court misinterpreted section 56–5–2953 of the South Carolina Code. We agree.

State law generally requires a person charged with DUI to have his conduct at the incident site recorded on video, including his performance of any field sobriety tests. S.C.Code Ann. § 56–5–2953(A) (Supp.2015).[1] However, subsection (B) of the statute creates exceptions to this general requirement:

> Failure by the arresting officer to produce the video recording required by this section is not alone a ground for dismissal of any charge made pursuant to [s]ection 56–5–2930, 56–5–2933, or 56–5–2945 if the arresting officer submits a sworn affidavit certifying that the video recording equipment at the time of the arrest or probable cause determination, or video equipment at the breath test facility was in an inoperable condition, stating which reasonable efforts have been made to maintain the equipment in an operable condition, and certifying that there was no other operable breath test facility available in the county or, in the alternative, submits a sworn affidavit certifying that it was physically impossible to produce the video recording because the person needed emergency medical treatment, or exigent circumstances existed. *In circumstances including, but not limited to, road blocks, traffic accident investigations, and citizens' arrests, where an arrest has been made and the video recording equipment has not been activated by blue lights, the failure by the arresting officer to produce the video recordings required by this section is not alone a ground for dismissal.* However, as soon as video recording is practicable in these circumstances, video recording must begin and conform with the provisions of this section. **\*175** *Nothing in this section prohibits the court from considering any other valid reason for the failure to produce the video recording based upon the totality of the circumstances;* nor do the provisions of this section prohibit the person from offering evidence relating to the arresting law enforcement officer's failure to produce the video recording.

*Id.* § 56–5–2953(B) (emphasis added).

Shortly before Respondent's trial, we held that failure to comply with the video-recording requirement justifies dismissal of a DUI charge, unless noncompliance is excused under subsection (B) above. *City of Rock Hill v. Suchenski,* 374 S.C. 12, 17, 646 S.E.2d 879, 881 (2007) (holding dismissal of a DUI charge "is an appropriate remedy provided by [section] 56–5–2953 where a violation of **111 subsection (A) is not mitigated by subsection (B) exceptions").

In the present case, Respondent's FSBL and felony DUI charges arose from a chain of events that began in the City of Spartanburg in the early morning hours of February 3, 2006. As Respondent drove out of the parking lot of a convenience store around 1:00 a.m., he pulled out in front of Officer Timothy St. Louis of the City of Spartanburg Department of Public Safety. Officer St. Louis began following Respondent's car because he noticed Respondent was driving with his headlights off and because Respondent threw a beer can out of his vehicle's window. Officer St. Louis activated his recording camera and initiated his blue lights, suspecting the driver may have been intoxicated.[2] However, Respondent did not stop and continued to drive erratically. Officer St. Louis turned off his lights and siren, pursuant to the city's "no chase" policy, and put out a "be on the lookout" (BOLO) alert to county and state officers that included a description of Respondent's car and license plate.

Moments later, Spartanburg County Sheriff's Deputy David Evett spotted a vehicle matching the description from the BOLO traveling with its headlights off. When Deputy Evett pulled close behind Respondent's vehicle to verify the license plate number before initiating a traffic stop (by activating his lights and siren), Respondent took off at a high rate of speed. Deputy Evett activated his lights and siren and pursued *176 Respondent, but at a distance, as Respondent continued to flee at a high rate of speed and without headlights.[3]

Deputy Evett lost sight of Respondent's vehicle, but came in sight of his vehicle just as the vehicle collided head-on with another vehicle.[4] After witnessing sparks from the collision, Deputy Evett radioed for back-up and medical assistance, then exited his patrol car and checked on both drivers. The driver of the other vehicle was seriously injured. Although Respondent was injured, he managed to crawl through the passenger-side window and attempted to flee on foot. Deputy Evett stopped Respondent. Respondent and the driver of the other vehicle were transported to the hospital. Deputy Evett never activated his video camera.

Lance Corporal Dwayne Darity of the South Carolina Highway Patrol responded to the hospital to investigate the accident. Corporal Darity believed Respondent was intoxicated because Respondent was uncooperative and smelled of alcohol. Corporal Darity charged Respondent with felony DUI but did not conduct any field sobriety tests because he suspected Respondent suffered serious injuries in the collision. Blood and urine samples collected from Respondent at the hospital revealed Respondent had marijuana and alcohol in his system at the time of the accident.[5] Marijuana was also found in the vehicle Respondent had been driving.

 The PCR court found that Respondent's trial counsel was deficient for not moving to dismiss the DUI charge because, as the PCR court posited, *Suchenski* established that an officer's failure to comply with the video-recording requirement **\*177** mandated dismissal of the charge. The PCR court also (erroneously) concluded that Respondent was prejudiced because, although subsection (B) of the statute excuses noncompliance with the recording requirement in certain situations, those exceptions require the arresting officer to submit a sworn affidavit. As no affidavit was submitted in this case, the PCR court concluded that the motion to dismiss **\*\*112** would have been granted and, therefore, trial counsel was ineffective.

The PCR court committed an error of law in interpreting subsection (B) to require an affidavit under all exceptions. The follow-up finding that the trial court would have likely granted a motion to dismiss the DUI charge, which was the basis for the PCR court's finding of prejudice, was therefore controlled by an error of law, and we reverse. *See Bryant v. State,* 384 S.C. 525, 528–29, 683 S.E.2d 280, 282 (2009) (citation

49

omitted) (stating statutory interpretation is a question of law, and this Court will reverse a PCR court's decision when it is controlled by an error of law).

We have previously interpreted the exceptions in subsection (B) to not require a sworn affidavit in all circumstances:

> Subsection (B) of section 56–5–2953 outlines several statutory exceptions that excuse noncompliance with the mandatory videotaping requirements. Noncompliance is excusable[ ](1) if the arresting officer submits a sworn affidavit certifying the video equipment was inoperable despite efforts to maintain it; (2) if the arresting officer submits a sworn affidavit that it was impossible to produce the videotape because the defendant either (a) needed emergency medical treatment or (b) exigent circumstances existed; (3) in circumstances including, but not limited to, road blocks, traffic accidents, and citizens' arrests; or (4) for any other valid reason for the failure to produce the videotape based upon the totality of the circumstances.

*Town of Mount Pleasant v. Roberts,* 393 S.C. 332, 346, 713 S.E.2d 278, 285 (2011). Thus, based on this Court's interpretation of the statute in *Roberts,* an affidavit is not needed to qualify for the third and fourth exceptions. As Respondent was arrested for FSBL in connection with a traffic accident, this case falls within the third exception.

**\*178** This Court has recently interpreted the third exception, regarding traffic accidents, to excuse the videotaping requirement only up to the point where videotaping becomes practicable. *State v. Henkel,* 413 S.C. 9, 14, 774 S.E.2d 458, 461 (2015). Here, because Respondent's vehicle's headlights were off, Deputy Evett could not see Respondent's vehicle until it collided with the other vehicle. Once the accident occurred, the urgency of the situation (calling for back-up, assessing injuries, and securing Respondent who was attempting to flee)
50

understandably became Deputy Evett's primary concerns. We further note Respondent was not suspected of DUI until Corporal Darity spoke with Respondent at the hospital.[6]

The failure to initiate videotaping in this case could also be excused under the totality of the circumstances, which is the fourth exception. As this Court recognized in *Henkel,* "Subsection (A) was intended to capture the interactions and field sobriety testing between the subject and the officer in a typical DUI traffic stop where there are no other witnesses." *Id.* (citing *Roberts,* 393 S.C. at 347, 713 S.E.2d at 285). This situation, created solely by Respondent's dangerous and evasive driving, does not resemble a typical traffic stop. As Respondent was pursued and arrested in connection with the FSBL charge and was not charged with felony DUI until after he was transported to the hospital, no field sobriety tests were administered or could have been captured on video. The legislative concerns with videotaping one-on-one traffic stops are not implicated under the facts of this case, and under the totality of the circumstances, Deputy Evett's failure to produce a videotape was reasonable and excusable.

Therefore, even if trial counsel was deficient in failing to move to dismiss the felony DUI charge based on the lack of videotape evidence, the prejudice prong required for an ineffective **\*179** assistance of counsel claim cannot be established. It was purely speculative for **\*\*113** the PCR court to conclude that the motion likely would have been granted. Perhaps more importantly, the prejudice finding was grounded in the erroneous finding that all subsection (B) exceptions require an affidavit. Under both the totality of the circumstances and the traffic-accident exception, neither of which require an affidavit, the trial court would not have abused its discretion in denying a motion to dismiss the DUI charge. Thus, we reverse the PCR court's grant of relief to Respondent on this ground.

## II.

The State next argues the PCR court erred in finding Respondent's trial counsel ineffective for failing to impeach one of the witnesses to the home invasion with a prior criminal conviction. While we hold there is evidence in the record to support the PCR court's finding that counsel was deficient, we nevertheless find the PCR court erred in finding this failure prejudiced Respondent.

Respondent was convicted of first-degree burglary in connection with his invasion of the home of his long-time neighbors—Mary Gray (Mary); Mary's two children, Erica Gray (Erica) and Donald Martin (Donald); and Mary's nine-year-old granddaughter, Javanica. At trial, Erica testified Respondent broke into the home, held her and her family at gunpoint, and robbed them. Mary, Donald, and Javanica also testified that Respondent broke into the home and robbed the family at gunpoint. Further, Officer Adrian Patton of the Spartanburg Department of Public Safety, who responded to the scene within minutes of the incident, testified the victims immediately identified Respondent as the intruder, even though he was wearing a ski mask, because they knew Respondent well and recognized his voice. At trial, defense counsel cross-examined Erica about her 1997 conviction for distributing crack-cocaine and cross-examined Donald about his 2002 conviction for drug distribution.

At the PCR hearing, Respondent introduced another conviction for Erica, a 1995 conviction for giving false information to police about a shooting and burglary that took place at her home. Trial counsel testified he received a printout of the **\*180** National Crime Information Center report on Erica before trial, and the report showed an arrest for giving false information; however, trial counsel testified he did not use this information to impeach Erica at trial because the report did not give a disposition for the charge.

The PCR court found trial counsel was deficient for failing to impeach Erica with her prior conviction for giving false information to police because the conviction was likely admissible under Rule 609(b), SCRE, governing the admission of prior convictions more than ten years old, and the balancing test in *State v. Colf,* 337 S.C. 622, 525 S.E.2d 246 (2000). The PCR court also found Respondent was prejudiced by this deficiency because Erica was an important witness in establishing

Respondent's identity as the intruder and impeachment of Erica with this conviction would have "directly affected" the outcome of the trial.

Although there is evidence to support the PCR court's finding that trial counsel was deficient for failing to impeach Erica with the prior conviction, we find the PCR court erred in finding Respondent was prejudiced because there is not a reasonable probability the impeachment of Erica would have directly affected the outcome of Respondent's trial. *See Dawkins v. State,* 346 S.C. 151, 156, 551 S.E.2d 260, 262 (2001) ("To show prejudice, the applicant must show, but for counsel's errors, there is a reasonable probability the result of the trial would have been different. A reasonable probability is a probability sufficient to undermine confidence in the outcome of trial." (citing *Brown v. State,* 340 S.C. 590, 593, 533 S.E.2d 308, 309–10 (2000))).

Specifically, many witnesses identified Respondent, for he was well known to Erica and the other witnesses. Also, defense counsel used Erica's distribution of crack-cocaine conviction for impeachment purposes. Moreover, Officer Patton testified that when he arrived on the scene, the victims immediately identified Respondent as the burglar. Therefore, there is no evidence to support the PCR court's finding that the additional impeachment of Erica would have undermined the evidence of Respondent's identity **114 as the intruder sufficient to create a reasonable probability that the jury would have found Respondent not guilty of burglary. *See Edwards v.* *181 *State,* 392 S.C. 449, 459, 710 S.E.2d 60, 66 (2011) (explaining that, to prevail, a PCR applicant "must show that the factfinder would have had a reasonable doubt respecting guilt" had the omitted evidence been introduced at trial and noting that no prejudice results from counsel's failure to bring forward cumulative evidence (citation and internal quotation marks omitted)); *Harris v. State,* 377 S.C. 66, 78, 659 S.E.2d 140, 147 (2008) (finding trial counsel's failure to impeach a witness who identified the accused as the perpetrator of the crime was " inconsequential" and not prejudicial where other evidence of identity was properly admitted at trial); *Huggler v. State,* 360 S.C. 627, 634–36, 602 S.E.2d 753, 757–58 (2004) (finding the PCR applicant was not prejudiced by trial counsel's failure to object to the introduction of the victims' written statements into evidence or trial counsel's alleged failure to adequately cross-examine witnesses where the State presented overwhelming evidence from four witnesses who testified in detail against the applicant). We therefore reverse the PCR court's granting of relief on this ground.

## III.

The State next argues the PCR court erred in finding trial counsel was ineffective for failing to move for a directed verdict on the burglary charge. We agree.

The PCR court concluded trial counsel was deficient in failing to move for a directed verdict because Respondent contended he had permission to enter the victims' home. *See* S.C.Code Ann. § 16–11–311(A) (2015) (defining first-degree burglary as, in part, entering a dwelling without consent). The PCR court also found Respondent was prejudiced because the directed verdict motion likely would have been granted. This was error.

As a matter of law, Respondent would not have been entitled to a directed verdict on the burglary charge. In ruling on a directed verdict motion, the trial court does not view the evidence in the light most favorable to the movant. *See, e.g., State v. Weston,* 367 S.C. 279, 292, 625 S.E.2d 641, 648 (2006) (explaining that when ruling on a motion for a directed verdict, the evidence must be viewed in a light favorable to the nonmoving party, and the trial court is *182 concerned only with the existence or nonexistence of evidence, not its weight); *State v. Prince,* 316 S.C. 57, 64, 447 S.E.2d 177, 181 (1993) ("[I]n ruling on a motion for directed verdict, the trial court must view the evidence in the light most favorable to the State.").

Viewing the evidence in the light most favorable to the State, ample evidence was presented to survive a directed verdict motion. For example, Donald testified that he heard a knock at the door, after which Respondent identified himself by his nickname. Donald stated he cracked the door, at which point Respondent forced open the door and pushed his way into the home while wielding a shotgun. Donald testified Respondent order him to take off his pants and shoes, and then took $500 from him. Properly viewing all the evidence in the light most favorable to the State, as a court must in evaluating a directed verdict motion, had a directed verdict motion been made, it would have been denied. *See Prince,* 316 S.C. at 64, 447 S.E.2d at 181–82 ("The case should be submitted to the jury if there is any substantial evidence which reasonably tends to prove the guilt of the accused or from which guilt may be fairly and logically deduced." (citations omitted)). We thus hold that the PCR court erred as a matter of law in finding Respondent's trial counsel was deficient for failing to move for a directed verdict on the burglary charge.

## IV.

 Finally, the State argues the PCR court erred in finding Respondent's trial counsel ineffective for failing to object to a portion of the trial court's jury instructions because no case law existed at the time of Respondent's trial that would have made the instruction objectionable. Again, we agree.

The trial court's charge to the jury included the following instruction: "Your sole objective of course is to simply reach the truth **115 in the matter, and by doing that you will have fulfilled your obligations as jurors, and that is to simply give both the [S]tate and [Respondent] a fair and impartial trial." Five years after Respondent's trial, this Court criticized a similar instruction: "This court is of the confirmed opinion *183 that whatever verdict you reach will represent truth and justice for all parties that are involved in this case." *State v. Daniels,* 401 S.C. 251, 254, 737 S.E.2d 473, 474 (2012) (internal quotation marks omitted). This Court ordered

> trial judge[s] to remove any suggestion from [their] general sessions charges that a criminal jury's duty is to return a verdict that is "just" or "fair" to all parties. Such a charge could effectively alter the

jury's perception of the burden of proof, substituting justice and fairness for the presumption of innocence and the State's burden to prove the defendant's guilt beyond a reasonable doubt. Moreover, to a lay person, the "all parties involved" in a criminal case may well extend beyond the defendant and the State, and include the victim. These inaccurate and misleading charges risk depriving a criminal defendant of his right to a fair trial.

*Id.* at 256, 737 S.E.2d at 475.

The PCR court found trial counsel was ineffective for failing to object to the trial court's instruction, even though *Daniels* had not yet been decided, because if trial counsel had made an objection, the issue would have been preserved for appellate review. The PCR court also found Respondent was prejudiced because the jury likely "relieved the State of its burden of proof."

We disagree and hold that the PCR court erred in finding trial counsel ineffective for failing to object to the jury instruction when no case law existed rendering the instruction improper per se. This Court has previously held that reasonable representation does not require trial counsel to foresee successful appellate challenges to novel questions of law. *E.g., Gilmore v. State,* 314 S.C. 453, 457, 445 S.E.2d 454, 456 (1994) ("We have never required an attorney to be clairvoyant or anticipate changes in the law...." (citing *Thornes v. State,* 310 S.C. 306, 309–10, 426 S.E.2d 764, 765 (1993))), *overruled on other grounds by Brightman v. State,* 336 S.C. 348, 520 S.E.2d 614 (1999); *Thornes,* 310 S.C. at 309–10, 426 S.E.2d at 765 ("This Court has never required an attorney to anticipate or discover changes in the law, or facts which did not exist, at the time of the trial."). As trial counsel's performance was not deficient, we reverse the PCR court's grant of relief on this ground.

**\*184 V.**

For the foregoing reasons, the PCR court's grant of relief to Respondent is reversed. Respondent's convictions and sentences are hereby reinstated.

**REVERSED.**

BEATTY, Acting Chief Justice, HEARN, J. and Acting Justice JEAN H. TOAL, concur.

PLEICONES, C.J., not participating.

**All Citations**

416 S.C. 171, 786 S.E.2d 109

Footnotes

[1] Although the statute has been amended since Respondent's arrest in 2006, the portions relevant to this case remained substantially the same. We therefore cite to the latest version of the statute.

[2] This video was introduced at trial.

[3] Respondent traveled in excess of seventy miles per hour in areas where the speed limit ranged from thirty-five to forty-five miles per hour.

[4] Respondent's headlights were off at the time of the collision.

[5] Respondent's blood alcohol content was below the legal limit; however, the State contended Respondent was nonetheless driving under the influence because blood tests indicated he had smoked marijuana within 90 minutes of the accident. The State's forensic toxicology expert testified that the amount of marijuana in Respondent's system would impair his ability to drive and that this impairment would be further exacerbated by the presence of any amount of alcohol, even an amount below the legal limit.

[6] Unlike Officer St. Louis, Deputy Evett began following Respondent because Respondent's vehicle matched the BOLO description of the vehicle that failed to stop for a blue light—not because he suspected Respondent of DUI. Deputy Evett testified he did not spend sufficient time with Respondent at the accident scene to suspect Respondent was under the influence of drugs or alcohol. Deputy Evett was dealing with a serious motor vehicle accident and was focused on ensuring those injured received prompt medical attention.

# _Henkel_

413 S.C. 9
Supreme Court of South Carolina.

The STATE, Petitioner,
v.
Gregg Gerald HENKEL, Respondent.

**Opinion**

Justice PLEICONES.

**\*10** We granted the State's petition for a writ of certiorari to review the Court of Appeals' opinion that found the trial court should have dismissed respondent's DUI charge because the videotape did not comply with the statutory requirements for videotaping respondent's conduct at the scene of his DUI arrest. _State v. Henkel,_ 404 S.C. 626, 746 S.E.2d 347 (Ct.App.2013); S.C.Code Ann. § 56–5–2953 (2006). We reverse.

## FACTS

A witness observed a vehicle being driven erratically on I–385 and ultimately wrecking. Sergeant Hiott responded to the wreck and organized a search after learning from a witness that the driver had fled the scene. Officers were unable to locate the driver and cleared the scene.

Several hours later, Sergeant Hiott responded to a call indicating an individual had been found walking down I–385. When Sergeant Hiott arrived, he found respondent receiving medical care in an ambulance. Sergeant Hiott read respondent *11 his *Miranda*[1] rights and conducted a horizontal gaze nystagmus (HGN) test while respondent was in the ambulance. Sergeant Hiott initiated his audio recording device by a switch on his belt during the HGN test.[2] After the HGN test, Sergeant Hiott learned **460 respondent was not going to the hospital, so he led respondent from the ambulance to the side of his vehicle and asked him to recite the alphabet. Respondent failed both the HGN and ABC tests.[3] The ABC test and Sergeant Hiott's admonitions while administering the HGN test were captured by audio recording. Neither test was captured by video recording. Sergeant Hiott arrested respondent for DUI, placed respondent in his patrol vehicle, faced the in-car camera towards respondent, and read respondent his *Miranda* rights again.

Respondent sought dismissal of the charge alleging the videotape of his conduct at the scene failed to comply with the statutory videotaping requirements. Subsection 56–5–2953 (A) requires that an individual have his conduct recorded at the incident site, and that the recording must include that individual being advised of his *Miranda* rights prior to the administration of field sobriety tests.[4] Subsection

*12 (B) provides several exceptions to this videotaping requirement:

> [I]n circumstances including, but not limited to, road blocks, traffic accident investigations, and citizens' arrests, where an arrest has been made and the videotaping equipment has not been activated by blue lights, the failure by the arresting officer to produce the videotapes required by this section is not alone a ground for dismissal. However, as soon as videotaping is practicable in these circumstances, videotaping must begin and conform with the provisions of this section.

S.C.Code Ann. § 56–5–2953(B) (2006).

The trial court denied respondent's motion to dismiss. The trial court recognized this incident was not a typical DUI stop because Sergeant

60

Hiott's investigation began hours after respondent's wreck. Accordingly, the trial court applied subsection (B), and found Sergeant Hiott activated the video and audio recording as soon as practicable.[5] The trial court found the videotape complied with the requirements of subsection (A) because it captured audio of the HGN and ABC tests.

The Court of Appeals reversed. The majority first looked to subsection (B) because the videotaping equipment was not activated by Sergeant Hiott's blue lights and Sergeant Hiott was conducting a traffic accident investigation. The majority applied the language of subsection (B) which provides two qualifying provisions: "[h]owever, as soon as videotaping is practicable in these circumstances, videotaping must begin and conform with the provisions of this section." S.C.Code Ann. § 56–5–2953(B). The majority found the language which requires "videotaping must begin and conform with the provisions of this section," necessitates compliance with subsection (A). That is, the majority held that once videotaping begins, it must include **all** the requirements of subsection (A). Subsection *13 (A)(1)(b) requires the videotaping "include the person being advised of his *Miranda* rights before any field sobriety tests are administered." Here, the first *Miranda* warning was not captured by audio or video. Accordingly, the majority found dismissal of the charge was required because the videotape did not capture respondent being advised of his *Miranda* rights before the audio **461 recording of the HGN and ABC tests.[6]

Judge Geathers dissented and reasoned that to require strict compliance with subsection (A)(1)(b) would effectively eviscerate the exception in subsection (B). Judge Geathers observed an officer is required to begin recording as soon as practicable, and the "begin and conform" provision in subsection (B) was intended to require compliance with subsection (A), *from that point forward.* Judge Geathers stated "the initiation of the videotaping and conformance must each begin as soon as is practicable," and here, it was not practicable to capture video evidence of respondent receiving his initial *Miranda* warnings or performing the HGN and ABC tests. Accordingly, Judge Geathers would have affirmed respondent's conviction and sentence.

## ISSUE

Did the videotape of respondent's conduct made at the scene of his traffic accident investigation comply with the videotaping requirements of S.C.Code Ann. § 56–5–2953, as it existed in January 2008?

## ANALYSIS

The State contends the Court of Appeals misapplied the exception in subsection (B) because the phrase "as soon as videotaping is practicable" applies to both when the videotaping must "begin" and what it must show in order to "conform" to the requirements of subsection (A). The State argues the effect of the Court of Appeals' opinion requires, in situations such as this, the arresting officer to perform *Miranda* warnings and field sobriety tests anew, in order to capture them on *14 videotape, if they were first performed prior to the moment where videotaping became practicable. We find the language of the exception in subsection (B) ambiguous, and construe the exception to require compliance with subsection (A) need only begin at the time videotaping becomes practicable, and continue until the arrest is complete.

"The primary rule of statutory construction is to ascertain and give effect to the intent of the legislature." *Bryant v. State,* 384 S.C. 525, 529, 683 S.E.2d 280, 282 (2009). However, "[a]ll rules of statutory construction are subservient to the one that the legislative intent must prevail if it can be reasonably discovered in the language used, and that language must be construed in light of the intended purpose of the statute." *State v. Sweat,* 386 S.C. 339, 350, 688 S.E.2d 569, 575 (2010).

If the statute is ambiguous, courts must construe the terms of the statute. *Lester v. S.C. Workers' Comp. Comm'n,* 334 S.C. 557, 561, 514 S.E.2d 751, 752 (1999). "A statute as a whole must receive practical, reasonable, and fair interpretation consonant with the purpose, design, and policy of lawmakers." *Sloan v. S.C. Bd. of Physical Therapy*

*Exam'rs,* 370 S.C. 452, 468, 636 S.E.2d 598, 606–07 (2006). We have strictly construed § 56–5–2953. *Town of Mt. Pleasant v. Roberts,* 393 S.C. 332, 346, 713 S.E.2d 278, 285 (2011).

We find the language of the exception in subsection (B) ambiguous and construe the exception to require compliance with subsection (A) when it becomes practicable to begin videotaping. Accordingly, we find Court of Appeals' majority erred, for two reasons, in finding once videotaping begins pursuant to an exception in subsection (B), that full compliance with subsection (A) is necessary. First, the majority opinion violates the legislative intent of the statute. Subsection (A) was intended to capture the interactions and field sobriety testing between the subject and the officer in a typical DUI traffic stop where there are no other witnesses. *Roberts,* 393 S.C. at 347, 713 S.E.2d at 285 (finding the purpose of § 56–5–2953 is to create direct evidence of a DUI arrest). During a traffic stop, the subject, his vehicle, and his interaction with the officer can be videotaped by the car-mounted camera that is initiated by the officer's blue lights. *15 Requiring an officer to repeat *Miranda* and field sobriety tests on camera in a situation contemplated in subsection **462 (B) is not consistent with the legislative intent of the DUI recording statute.

Here, the legislative concerns with videotaping one-on-one traffic stops to capture the interactions between an officer and the subject are not present. *See Sweat,* 386 S.C. at 350, 688 S.E.2d at 575 (holding "language must be construed in light of the intended purpose of the statute."). Numerous officers and emergency personnel observed respondent's conduct at the scene. Officer Hamilton testified he was the first responder that located respondent walking down I–385. Officer Hamilton testified respondent was unsteady on his feet, he was confused, and he was talking with a slurred voice. Officer Terry testified he also responded to the call reporting that respondent was walking down I–385 and he believed respondent was definitely intoxicated. He explained respondent was slurring his speech, his posture was slumped over, and he smelled like alcohol.

Second, the majority opinion fails to consider the statute as a whole.

*Mid–State Auto Auction of Lexington, Inc. v. Altman,* 324 S.C. 65, 69, 476 S.E.2d 690, 692 (1996) ("In ascertaining the intent of the legislature, a court should not focus on any single section or provision but should consider the language of the statute as a whole."). In effect, the majority opinion would render the exceptions for road blocks, traffic accident investigations, and citizens' arrests meaningless, if during an encounter it becomes practicable to begin videotaping. The majority requires an arresting officer to repeat *Miranda* warnings and field sobriety tests if it becomes practicable to begin videotaping; especially when, as occurred here, *Miranda* and a portion of a field sobriety test were conducted prior to the moment when videotaping became practicable. We hold the phrase "as soon as videotaping is practicable in these circumstances," applies to both when videotaping must "begin" and when videotaping must "conform to the provisions of this section."

Accordingly, we hold when an individual's conduct is videotaped during a situation provided for in subsection (B), compliance with subsection (A) must begin at the time videotaping **\*16** becomes practicable and continue until the arrest is complete. Subsection (A) of the statute as it existed at the time of respondent's arrest only required respondent's conduct be videotaped and *Miranda* warnings be given prior to field sobriety tests. We find the audio recording of respondent's field sobriety tests adequately captured his conduct at the scene of the traffic accident investigation. Additionally, because respondent was given *Miranda* warnings prior to the time videotaping became practicable, we hold the videotape complies with subsection (A) because the videotape need only begin complying with subsection (A) from the time videotaping became practicable. *See* footnote 5, *supra.*

We reverse the Court of Appeals and reinstate respondent's conviction because the videotape satisfied the requirements of § 56–5–2953 once videotaping became practicable.[7]

## CONCLUSION

For the reasons given above, the opinion of the Court of Appeals is

Reversed.


TOAL, C.J., BEATTY, KITTREDGE and HEARN, JJ., concur.

**All Citations**

413 S.C. 9, 774 S.E.2d 458

Footnotes

[1]  *Miranda v. Arizona,* 384 U.S. 436, 86 S.Ct. 1602, 16 L.Ed.2d 694 (1966).

[2]  This switch also activated patrol car's video recording camera. This forward facing camera only recorded the highway in front of Sergeant Hiott's vehicle. When Sergeant Hiott arrived at the scene, he pulled his patrol vehicle past all of the other emergency vehicles.

[3]  No balancing tests were administered because respondent indicated he had an injured leg.

[4]  Subsection (A) states:
     (A) A person who violates Section 56–5–2930, 56–5–2933, or 56–5–2945 must have his conduct at the incident site and the breath test site videotaped.
     (1) The videotaping at the incident site must:
     (a) begin not later than the activation of the officer's blue lights and conclude after the arrest of the person for a violation of Section 56–5–2930, 56–5–2933, or a probable cause determination that the person violated Section 56–5–2945; and
     (b) include the person being advised of his *Miranda* rights before any field sobriety tests are administered, if the tests are administered.
     We note that § 56–5–2953 was amended effective February 10, 2009. *See* Act No. 201, 2008 S.C. Acts 1682–85. While subsection (A) was amended, the language of subsection (B) was essentially unchanged. Respondent's arrest occurred on January 19, 2008, so the amended statute is not applicable.

5   The trial court's factual finding that videotaping began as soon as practicable is not challenged on appeal.

6   This same issue will not arise under the amended version of the statute because while it requires both the field sobriety tests and the *Miranda* rights be recorded, it does not require *Miranda* rights be given **before** the field sobriety tests.

# _Suchenski_

374 S.C. 12
Supreme Court of South Carolina.

The CITY OF ROCK HILL, Appellant,
v.
Cynthia A. SUCHENSKI, Respondent.

**Opinion**

Acting Justice MANNING:

**\*14** This is an appeal from the Rock Hill municipal court. Cynthia Suchenski (respondent) was found guilty of driving with an unlawful alcohol concentration (DUAC), and the circuit court reversed her conviction based on the City of Rock Hill's (City's) failure to comply with S.C.Code Ann. § 56-5-2953 (2006), which requires the arresting officer to provide videotaping of the incident site. We affirm.

## FACTS

Respondent was arrested for driving under the influence (DUI) and was later charged with DUAC. At the incident site, the arresting officer did not videotape the entire arrest as required by § 56-5-2953 because the officer's camera ran out of tape. The videotaping began upon activation of the officer's blue lights and recorded two field sobriety tests and the _Miranda_ warnings, but the tape stopped before the officer administered a third field sobriety test and before respondent was arrested.

At trial, respondent moved to dismiss the charges due to the officer's failure to provide a complete videotape from the incident site. The officer testified that a tape had never ended during an arrest before and that he turned on his blue lights and assumed the **880 videotape was running as usual. The officer stated he did not know the tape was about to expire. The municipal court denied the motion pursuant to the statute on the grounds of exigent circumstances. The municipal court also cited *State v. Huntley,* 349 S.C. 1, 562 S.E.2d 472 (2002), and *State v. Mabe,* 306 S.C. 355, 412 S.E.2d 386 (1991), in support of its denial of respondent's motion to dismiss.

The case was tried before a jury, and respondent was found guilty. Respondent appealed her conviction, and the circuit court reversed, holding that respondent's motion to dismiss should have been granted. The circuit court distinguished *Huntley* and *Mabe,* the two cases relied upon by the municipal court in denying respondent's motion to dismiss. However, the circuit court did not address the finding of the municipal court that exigent circumstances excused compliance with the statute and simply held that the City violated the videotaping statute.

## *15 ISSUE

Did the circuit court err in reversing respondent's conviction and dismissing the DUAC charge?

## ANALYSIS

In criminal appeals from municipal court, the circuit court does not conduct a de novo review. S.C.Code Ann. § 14-25-105 (Supp.2006); *State v. Landis,* 362 S.C. 97, 606 S.E.2d 503 (Ct.App.2004). In criminal cases, the appellate court reviews errors of law only. *State v. Cutter,* 261 S.C. 140, 199 S.E.2d 61 (1973). Therefore, our scope of review is limited to correcting the circuit court's order for errors of law.

The City first argues that the circuit court erred by determining the City

68

violated S.C.Code Ann. § 56-5-2953. This issue is not preserved.

Section 56-5-2953 commands the arresting officer to videotape the individual during a DUI arrest. Subsection (A) of the statute outlines the requirements for videotaping at the incident site and at the breath test site. Subsection (B) of the statute provides exceptions that excuse compliance with the statute.[1] In this case, both parties agreed that the arresting officer failed to comply with the requirements of subsection (A), but the municipal court denied respondent's motion to dismiss due to an exception in subsection (B).

On appeal to the circuit court, the City reiterated its position that noncompliance was excused pursuant to § 56-5-2953(B). However, the circuit court's order did not address or even mention the exceptions in subsection (B). The circuit court simply concluded, "Here, the legislature has established a procedure that *must* be followed in the making of a DUI arrest. Here, the procedure was not followed." While the circuit court correctly applied subsection (A) of the statute, it omitted any mention of subsection (B) of § 56-5-2953.

**\*16** The City did not seek a post-judgment ruling from the circuit court on the potential applicability of § 56-5-2953(B). This precludes our review of the applicability of the subsection (B) exceptions, as we may only review the circuit court's order for errors of law. We cannot determine error regarding an issue not addressed by the circuit court. *See Williams v. Williams,* 329 S.C. 569, 579, 496 S.E.2d 23, 29 (Ct.App.1998), *rev'd on other grounds,* 335 S.C. 386, 517 S.E.2d 689 (1999) ("The circuit court has the authority to hear motions to alter or amend the judgment when it sits in an appellate capacity, and these motions are required in order to preserve issues for further review by the Court of Appeals or the Supreme Court in cases where the circuit court fails to address an issue raised by a party."); *United Dominion Realty Trust, Inc. v. Wal-Mart Stores, Inc.,* 307 S.C. 102, 413 S.E.2d 866 (Ct.App.1992) (circuit court sitting on appeal did not address an issue and Wal-Mart made no motion pursuant to Rule 59(e), SCRCP, to have the court rule on the issue; thus the allegation was not preserved for further review by the Court of Appeals).

The City next contends that, per *Huntley,* a violation of the videotaping statute should not result in dismissal of a charge **\*\*881** when there was no showing of prejudice to the defendant. We disagree.

Under § 56-5-2953, a violation of the statute, with no mention of prejudice, may result in dismissal of the charges. The statute provides, "Failure by the arresting officer to produce the videotapes required by this section **is not alone a ground for dismissal** of any charge made pursuant to Section 56-5-2930, 56-5-2933, or 56-5-2945 **if** [exceptions apply] ..." (emphasis added). Conversely, failure to produce videotapes would be a ground for dismissal if no exceptions apply.

The circuit court found *Huntley* to be inapposite, and we agree. The statute at issue in *Huntley* was the implied consent statute which required a simulator test before administration of a breath test. That statute, S.C.Code Ann. § 56-5-2950 (2006), is silent as to the remedy for noncompliance, whereas the statute in this case provides for dismissal of charges when the statute is inexcusably violated.


## *17 CONCLUSION

The City failed to seek a ruling in the circuit court in regards to the applicability of the exceptions for noncompliance found in § 56-5-2953(B). Accordingly, that issue is not properly before us. Finally, dismissal of the DUAC charge is an appropriate remedy provided by § 56-5-2953 where a violation of subsection (A) is not mitigated by subsection (B) exceptions.

**AFFIRMED.**

MOORE, ACJ, WALLER, J., and Acting Justice JAMES W. JOHNSON, JR., concur. BURNETT, J., dissenting in a separate opinion.

BURNETT, J., dissenting:

I respectfully dissent. In my opinion, the issue of whether the circuit erred by determining the City violated S.C.Code Ann. § 56-5-2953 is preserved.

In order to preserve an issue for appellate review, a party must file a motion to alter or amend the judgment when the party raises an issue to the lower court and the court fails to rule upon the issue. *E.g., Elam v. South Carolina Dep't of Transp.,* 361 S.C. 9, 602 S.E.2d 772 (2004); *I'On, L.L.C. v. Town of Mt. Pleasant,* 338 S.C. 406, 526 S.E.2d 716 (2000); *see also* Rules 52(b) and 59(e), SCRCP. However, a motion to alter or amend the judgment under Rule 59(e) was not necessary in this case. Appellant's failure to move to seek a ruling from the lower court on the applicability of S.C.Code Ann. § 56-5-2953(B) (2006) does not violate the long-established preservation requirements.

Both parties argued the applicability of subsections (A) and (B) extensively in their briefs and at the hearing before the lower court. The lower court's determination hinged on whether subsection (B) provided an excuse for the violation of subsection (A). The lower court determined no exception in subsection (B) applied. Although the lower court's order only addressed subsection (A), the fact that subsection (B) did not apply was implicit in the order and, therefore, preserved for review.

*18 A preservation issue did not arise when the lower court implicitly ruled in the negative that no exception applied, as opposed to alternatively ruling in the positive that an exception applied. For preservation purposes, it was unnecessary for the lower court to rule upon an exception when no such exception applied. Hence, despite the fact the entire opinion addressed only subsection (A), Appellant was free to argue on appeal an exception in subsection (B) applied.

Section 56-5-2953(B), states, in pertinent part:

> Failure by the arresting officer to produce the videotapes required by this section is not alone a ground for dismissal of any charge made pursuant to Section 56-5-2930, 56-5-2933, or 56-5-2945 if the arresting officer submits a sworn affidavit certifying that the videotape equipment at the time of the arrest ... was in an inoperable condition, ... or in the alternative ... it was physically impossible to produce the videotape because the person needed emergency medical treatment, or **exigent circumstances existed.**

(emphasis added). In the instant case, the videotape began upon activation of the officer's blue lights and recorded two field sobriety tests and the *Miranda* warnings. The tape stopped before the officer administered a third field sobriety test and a "walk and **882 turn" test, and before Respondent was arrested. The officer testified he assumed the videotape was running as usual and did not know the tape had expired prematurely. The municipal court correctly denied Respondent's motion to dismiss based on the "exigent circumstances" exception in subsection (B).

Because it was unnecessary for Appellant to make a motion pursuant to Rule 59(e), the issue of whether subsection (B) applied is preserved for review. Accordingly, I would reverse the lower court and reinstate the decision of the municipal court.

Footnotes

[1] Respondent argues the applicable statutory provision states, "Nothing in this section prohibits the court from considering any other valid reason for the failure to produce the videotape based upon the totality of the circumstances."

# *Gordon*

414 S.C. 94
Supreme Court of South Carolina.

The STATE, Petitioner,

v.

Cody Roy GORDON, Respondent.

**Opinion**

Justice BEATTY.

**\*96** The State appeals the Court of Appeals' affirmation of the circuit court's interpretation of section 56–5–2953 of the South Carolina Code. The Court of Appeals found that section 56–5–2953 requires officers to record the head of the motorist when administering the Horizontal Gaze Nystagmus (HGN) field sobriety test and that Cody Gordon's head was not sufficiently visible. The State posits that a plain reading of the statute makes no mention of the motorist's "head." We affirm the Court of Appeals' conclusion that the statute requires that the motorist's head be recorded in the video; however, we vacate the mandate to remand to the magistrate court for further consideration. We reinstate Gordon's conviction as we find that the officer complied with the statute in recording Gordon's HGN test.

## I. Factual/Procedural History

On October 29, 2011, Gordon was stopped at a license and registration checkpoint by a South Carolina Highway Patrol

Officer. The officer administered several field sobriety tests. **\*97**
The test at issue in this case is the HGN test. The dashboard
camera on the officer's patrol car recorded the entire incident,
including all field sobriety tests, with continuous recording. The
stop occurred at night, so the lighting was not perfect, but the
officer had Gordon stand in the light of his patrol car's headlights
and further illuminated Gordon by shining a flashlight directly on
his face.

Following the tests, Gordon was placed under arrest. Gordon was
charged with driving under the influence (DUI) for violating
section 56–5–2930. The case was presented to a magistrate judge
and a jury. The jury found Gordon guilty as charged. Gordon
timely appealed his conviction.

Using still-shot photos of the video, Gordon argued that the video
violated section 56–5–2953(A) because he was out of sight and
in the dark during the HGN test. The circuit court concluded that
section 56–5–2953(A) requires the motorist's head to be visible
during the administration of the HGN field sobriety test. Section
56–5–2953(A) reads in pertinent part:

(A) A person who violates Section 56–5–2930, 56–5–2933, or
56–5–2945 must have his *conduct* at the incident site and
breath test site video recorded.

(1)(a) The video recording at the incident site must:

(i) not begin later than the activation of the officer's blue
lights;

(ii) *include any field sobriety tests administered;* and

(iii) include the arrest of a person for violation of Section 56–
5–2930 or Section 56–5–2933, or a probable cause
determination in that the person violated Section 56–5–2945,

74

and show the person being advised of his Miranda rights.

S.C.Code Ann. § 56–5–2953(A) (Supp.2011) (emphasis added). The circuit court found Gordon's head was not "sufficiently visible through the entire administration of the [HGN] test." The circuit court reversed his conviction and dismissed the DUI charge. The State timely appealed to the Court of Appeals.

**378 The Court of Appeals affirmed in part, vacated in part, and remanded the case to the magistrate court. *State v. Gordon,* 408 S.C. 536, 759 S.E.2d 755 (Ct.App.2014). The court concluded *98 that "the circuit court correctly found the head must be shown during the HGN test in order for that sobriety test to be recorded, and we affirm that finding." *Gordon,* 408 S.C. at 543, 759 S.E.2d at 758. The Court of Appeals remanded the case to the magistrate court with the instruction to "make factual findings in light of the circuit court and our determination that the test must be recorded on the camera; specifically for the HGN test, the head has to be visible on the recording." *Gordon,* 408 S.C. at 543–44, 759 S.E.2d at 759.

The Court of Appeals denied the State's petition for a rehearing.[1] This Court granted the State's petition for a writ of certiorari to review the Court of Appeals' decision.

## II. Standard of Review

In criminal cases, the appellate court sits to review errors of law only. *State v. Baccus,* 367 S.C. 41, 48, 625 S.E.2d 216, 220 (2006). Thus, an appellate court is bound by the trial court's factual findings unless they are clearly erroneous. *Id.*

"The cardinal rule of statutory interpretation is to ascertain and effectuate the intention of the legislature." *Sloan v. Hardee,* 371 S.C. 495, 498, 640 S.E.2d 457, 459 (2007). "When a statute's terms are clear and unambiguous on their face, there is no room for statutory construction and a court must apply the statute according to its literal meaning." *Id.* In interpreting a statute, "[w]ords must be given their plain and ordinary meaning without resort to subtle or forced construction to limit or expand the statute's operation." *Id.* at 499, 640 S.E.2d at 459.

## III. Discussion

**Whether the Court of Appeals erred in affirming the circuit court's decision to reverse Gordon's magistrate court conviction for driving under the influence?**

## *99 A. Argument

The State argues the Court of Appeals misconstrued the decision of the magistrate as lacking sufficient findings of fact. Specifically, the State contends that the Court of Appeals "misapprehended or overlooked the clear and unambiguous language of the statute, which does not include any requirement that 'the head must be visible on the recording' of an HGN field sobriety test."

## B. Analysis

The State would have us review this case using the analytical framework of *Murphy v. State,* 392 S.C. 626, 709 S.E.2d 685 (Ct.App.2011). The court in *Murphy* held that section 56–5–2953 only requires that the conduct of the motorist be recorded. *Murphy,* 392 S.C. at 631, 709 S.E.2d at 688. The Court of Appeals and the circuit court correctly distinguished *Murphy* from Gordon's case. In *Murphy,* the prior version of the statute at issue in this case was in effect. The prior version of the statute did not include the explicit requirement that the videotape include "any field sobriety tests administered." S.C.Code Ann. § 56–5–2953(A)(1)(a)(ii)(Supp.2011). The current version of the statute, which applies to Gordon, specifically requires that the officer record "any field sobriety tests administered." Based on this distinction, the magistrate erred as a matter of law in finding that the officer's recording was only required to show Gordon's conduct generally.

The statute at issue in this case is clear and unambiguous and, therefore, this Court must give its words their ordinary meaning. The statute states that the video recording "must include any field sobriety test administered," which necessarily includes the HGN test. Considering the fact that the HGN test focuses on eye movement, common sense dictates that the head must be visible on the video. Accordingly, the circuit court's finding that the head must be visible does not amount to a hyper-technicality, but merely states the obvious. The Court of **379** Appeals did not err in affirming this requirement.

Here, the officer's administration of the HGN test is visible on the video recording. It is undisputed that Gordon's *100** face is depicted in the video; it is axiomatic that the face is a part of the head. The officer's flashlight and arm are visible as he administers the test. Also, the officer's instructions were audible. Thus, the requirement that the head be visible on the video is met and the statutory requirement that the administration of the HGN field sobriety test be video recorded is satisfied. Therefore, the per se dismissal of the charge as discussed in *Town of Mount Pleasant v. Roberts,* 393 S.C. 332, 713 S.E.2d 278 (2011), and *City of Rock Hill v. Suchenski,* 374 S.C. 12, 646 S.E.2d 879 (2007) is not appropriate.

Even if we assume that the video of a field sobriety test is of such poor quality that its admission is more prejudicial than probative, the remedy would not be to dismiss the DUI charge. Instead, the remedy would be to redact the field sobriety test from the video and exclude testimony about the test.[2] If that remedy is applied here, there is still sufficient evidence to present this case to a jury for resolution. The evidence included the breath alcohol analysis report, video of other field sobriety tests, and Gordon's statement that he had consumed four beers.

Neither Gordon nor the State would have been prejudiced by the exclusion of the HGN test video or testimony because of the alleged poor quality of the video. Since the focus of the HGN test is the movement of the eyes, the jury would not have been able to determine if Gordon passed or failed by simply looking at this video. Moreover, the viewing of a video of an HGN field sobriety test has very little probative value to a jury because the eyes of the motorist are rarely, if ever, seen.[3]

The remaining issues raised by Gordon concerning discrepancies with the breath test site video's date and time stamp are without merit.

## IV. Conclusion

The Court of Appeals' decision is affirmed as to the requirements for video recording the HGN field sobriety test. The mandate to remand to the magistrate court for further consideration is vacated. Gordon's conviction is reinstated.

**\*101** TOAL, C.J., HEARN, J., and Acting Justice ALISON RENEE LEE, concur. PLEICONES, J., concurring in result only.

Footnotes

[1]   Additionally, the Court of Appeals withdrew its original opinion and substituted a new published one. *Gordon,* 408 S.C. at 536, 759 S.E.2d at 755.

[2]   It appears the solicitor unintentionally led the circuit court to believe that the HGN test was the only evidence against Gordon.

[3]   Of course, this would not be the case if actual eye movement is recorded.

# _Taylor_

411 S.C. 294
Court of Appeals of South Carolina.

The STATE, Appellant,
v.
Bailey TAYLOR, Respondent.

**Opinion**


KONDUROS, J.


*297 The magistrate court dismissed Bailey Taylor's charge for driving under the influence (DUI) because the required video recording of the incident site omitted Taylor from view for a period of time while the arresting officer repositioned his vehicle. The State appealed the circuit court's upholding of this dismissal. We reverse and remand.


**\*298 FACTS**
On July 22, 2011, South Carolina Highway Patrol Trooper E.S. Tolley charged Taylor with driving with unlawful alcohol concentration under section 56–5–2933 of the South Carolina Code (Supp.2013).[1] During the stop, as Tolley repositioned his patrol vehicle, the camera omitted Taylor from view for a period of time.

Taylor moved pretrial to dismiss the charge against her, arguing Tolley failed to comply with section 56–5–2953 of the South Carolina Code (Supp.2013)[2] because the video omitted her from view for several seconds and Tolley failed to submit an affidavit explaining why her actions were not recorded during that time. The State argued the officer was not required to capture all of the defendant's actions to satisfy the statute's requirements. The magistrate court dismissed Taylor's charge for driving with unlawful alcohol concentration. The magistrate court concluded the statute required the arresting officer to record all of

Taylor's conduct at the incident site and required the submission of an affidavit explaining why all of her conduct was not video recorded. The magistrate court concluded dismissal of Taylor's charge was an appropriate remedy when the State did not comply with the statute because Taylor's actions while outside the view of the video constituted "conduct," and Tolley failed to submit an affidavit. The magistrate's return does not contain any findings of fact other than stating Taylor's actions are omitted from view on the video for a period of time.[3]

The State appealed to the circuit court, arguing the magistrate court erred because the video recording captured all of the requirements of section 56–5–2953, even though the video omitted Taylor's actions at the incident site for several seconds. The State asserted the statute only specifically requires *299 certain aspects of the defendant's conduct at the incident site be recorded and the word "conduct" in the statute is not meant to encompass every action of the defendant. The State also contended its production of a video recording that met the requirements of the statute rendered the submission of an affidavit unnecessary. The circuit court affirmed the magistrate court, concluding the omission of Taylor's actions from view for several seconds violated the statute and Tolley failed to submit an affidavit but, finding the video began upon activation of blue lights, continuously recorded the entire time, captured all of the field sobriety tests administered, included Taylor's arrest, and showed Tolley advising Taylor of her **74 *Miranda*[4] rights.[5] This appeal followed.

## STANDARD OF REVIEW

"In criminal cases, the appellate court sits to review errors of law only." *State v. Baccus,* 367 S.C. 41, 48, 625 S.E.2d 216, 220 (2006). Thus, an appellate court is bound by the trial court's factual findings unless they are clearly erroneous. *Id.*

"In criminal appeals from magistrate ... court, the circuit court does not conduct a *de novo* review, but instead reviews for preserved error raised to it by appropriate exception." *State v. Henderson,* 347 S.C. 455, 457, 556 S.E.2d 691, 692 (Ct.App.2001); S.C.Code Ann. § 18–3–70 (Supp.2013) ("The appeal [from a magistrate in a criminal case] must be heard by the Court of Common Pleas upon the grounds of exceptions made and upon the papers required under this chapter, without the examination of witnesses in that court. And the court may either confirm the sentence appealed from, reverse or modify it, or grant a new trial, as to the court may seem meet and conformable to law."). This court will review **\*300** the decision of the magistrate court for errors of law only. *City of Rock Hill v. Suchenski,* 374 S.C. 12, 15, 646 S.E.2d 879, 880 (2007); *Henderson,* 347 S.C. at 457, 556 S.E.2d at 692.

In criminal appeals from the magistrate court, the circuit court is bound by the magistrate court's findings of fact if any evidence in the record reasonably supports them. *See City of Greer v. Humble,* 402 S.C. 609, 613, 742 S.E.2d 15, 17 (Ct.App.2013). "Moreover, [q]uestions of statutory interpretation are questions of law, which are subject to *de novo* review and which we are free to decide without any deference to the court below." *Id.* (alteration by court).

## LAW/ANALYSIS
The State contends the magistrate court and circuit court erred in dismissing the DUI charge under section 56–5–2953(A) of the South Carolina Code (Supp.2013) when the video recording briefly omitted Taylor from its view at the incident site but otherwise complied with the statute's requirements and when Tolley did not submit an affidavit explaining Taylor's omission from view. We agree.

"The cardinal rule of statutory construction is to ascertain and give effect to the intent of the legislature." *State v. Elwell,* 403 S.C. 606, 612, 743 S.E.2d 802, 806 (2013) (internal quotation marks omitted). "What a legislature says in the text of a statute is considered the best evidence of the legislative intent or will." *Id.* "Therefore, [i]f a statute's language is plain, unambiguous, and conveys a clear meaning[,] the rules of statutory interpretation are not needed and the court has no right to impose another meaning." *Id.* (internal quotation marks omitted); *see also State v. Pittman,* 373 S.C. 527, 561, 647 S.E.2d 144, 161 (2007) ("All rules of statutory construction are subservient to the maxim that legislative intent must prevail if it can be reasonably discovered in the language used."). "However, penal statutes will be strictly construed against the [S]tate." *Elwell,* 403 S.C. at 612, 743 S.E.2d at 806.

"If the statute is ambiguous, however, courts must construe the terms of the statute." *Town of Mt. Pleasant v. Roberts,* 393 S.C. 332, 342, 713 S.E.2d 278, 283 (2011). "A ***301** statute as a whole must receive a practical, reasonable, and fair interpretation consonant with the purpose, design, and policy of the lawmakers." *State v. Sweat,* 379 S.C. 367, 376, 665 S.E.2d 645, 650 (Ct.App.2008), *aff'd as modified,* 386 S.C. 339, 688 S.E.2d 569 (2010). "In interpreting a statute, the language of the statute must be read in a sense that harmonizes with its subject matter and accords with its general purpose." ****75** *Town of Mt. Pleasant,* 393 S.C. at 342, 713 S.E.2d at 283. "Any ambiguity in a statute should be resolved in favor of a just, equitable, and beneficial operation of the law." *Id.* (internal quotation marks omitted). "Courts will reject a statutory interpretation that would lead to a result so plainly absurd that it could not have been intended by the Legislature or would defeat the plain legislative intention." *Id.* at 342–43, 713 S.E.2d at 283.

A person who commits a DUI offense "must have his conduct at the incident site ... video recorded." § 56–5–2953(A). "The video recording at the incident site must: (i) not begin later than the activation of the officer's blue lights; (ii) include any field sobriety tests administered; and (iii) include the arrest of a person for a violation of ... [s]ection 56–5–2933[6] [of the South Carolina Code (Supp.2013) ], ... and show the person being advised of his [*Miranda* ] rights." § 56–5–2953(A)(1)(a)(i–iii). A violation of this section may result in dismissal of the DUI charges. S.C.Code Ann. § 56–5–2953(B) (Supp.2013); *see also City of Rock Hill v. Suchenski,* 374 S.C. 12, 17, 646 S.E.2d 879, 881 (2007) (holding dismissal of DUI charge is an appropriate remedy if the officer fails to produce a satisfactory video recording unless an exception applies).

In *Suchenski,* our supreme court affirmed the reversal of the defendant's DUI conviction when the video stopped recording before the officer administered a third field sobriety test and before the defendant was arrested. 374 S.C. at 14, 646 S.E.2d at 879. The City conceded the officer did not comply with the video recording requirement but asserted it was excused under section 56–5–2953(B). *Id.* at 14–15, 646 S.E.2d at 879–880. The court found the applicability of the exceptions unpreserved because the City failed to seek a post- **\*302** judgment ruling after the circuit court did not address section 56–5–2953(B) in its order. *Id.* at 15–16, 646 S.E.2d at 880. In applying the prior version of the statute, which required video recording to begin upon activation of blue lights and conclude after the defendant's arrest but did not specifically require video recording of field sobriety tests, the court held the City's failure to comply with the statute required dismissal of the charges. *Id.* at 14, 17, 646 S.E.2d at 879, 881; *see also* S.C.Code Ann. § 5–65–2953(A)(1) (2006).

In *Murphy v. State,* which the State asserts is controlling in this case, this court affirmed the defendant's DUI conviction under the prior version of the statute even though she conducted the horizontal gaze nystagmus (HGN)[7] test with her back to the vehicle camera and even though the video only recorded the defendant from the knees up as she performed the walk and turn test[8], occasionally only displaying half of her body. 392 S.C. 626, 628–29, 709 S.E.2d 685, 686–87 (Ct.App.2011). The defendant argued "the videotape of the incident [s]ite d[id] not comply with the statute because it fail[ed] to 'record most of the field sobriety tests.' " *Id.* at 631, 709 S.E.2d at 688. The court found "the plain language of the statute does not require that the recording capture a continuous full view of the accused, or capture *all* field sobriety tests. Rather, provided all other requirements are met, the video **\*303** need only record the accused's conduct." *Id.* at 632, 709 S.E.2d at 688. Further, the court concluded **\*\*76** "an unbroken recording of the tests is not necessary to capture conduct." *Id.* However, unlike the current statute, the statute applicable in *Murphy* did not include the explicit requirement that it "include any field sobriety tests administered."[9] § 56–5–2953(A)(1)(a)(ii). Instead, the statute only required the video recording to "include the person being advised of his *Miranda* rights before any field sobriety tests are administered, if the tests are administered." § 56–5–2953(A)(1)(b) (2006).

In *State v. Gordon,* the court of appeals affirmed the circuit court's determination that the statute required the HGN field sobriety test to be on video and specifically for the HGN test, the defendant's head must be on video. 408 S.C. 536, 543, 759 S.E.2d 755, 758 (Ct.App.2014), *cert. granted.* In *Gordon,* the defendant moved to dismiss the charge in magistrate court, arguing the State violated the statute because the video recording did not show his head during the administration of the HGN test. *Id.* at 539, 759 S.E.2d at 756. The magistrate court denied the motion under *Murphy*, finding the statute only required the defendant's conduct to be recorded, and the defendant was convicted in a jury trial. *Id.* The circuit court reversed his conviction on appeal, finding the defendant's head was not on video, which violated the statute. *Id.* at 539–40, 759 S.E.2d at 756–57. This court agreed the HGN test, specifically the defendant's head during the HGN test, must be recorded to comply with the statute. *Id.* at 543–44, 759 S.E.2d at 758–59. The court distinguished *Murphy* because, unlike the amended statute applicable in *Gordon* and in the present case, it was based on the prior statute, which did not specifically require video of the field sobriety tests. *Id.* at 543, 759 S.E.2d at 758; *see also* § 56–5–2953(A)(1)(a)(ii) (Supp.2013); § 56–5–2953(A)(1)(b) (2006). However, the court vacated the circuit court's factual finding that the defendant's head could not be seen on video because the circuit court may not make factual findings when sitting in an appellate capacity. *Gordon,* 408 S.C. at 543, 759 S.E.2d at 759. This court **\*304** then remanded to the magistrate court to determine whether the defendant's head was on the video recording because the magistrate court had never made any findings due to its misconstruction of the statute. *Id.* at 543–44, 759 S.E.2d at 759.

Dismissal of a DUI "charge is an appropriate remedy provided by section 56–5–2953 where a violation of subsection (A) is not mitigated by subsection (B) exceptions." *Suchenski,* 374 S.C. at 17, 646 S.E.2d at 881. "[T]he Legislature clearly intended for a *per se* dismissal in the event a law enforcement agency violates the mandatory provisions of section 56–5–2953." *Town of Mt. Pleasant,* 393 S.C. at 348, 713 S.E.2d at 286. "By requiring a law enforcement agency to videotape a DUI arrest, the Legislature clearly intended strict compliance with the provisions of section 56–5–2953 and, in turn, promulgated a severe sanction for noncompliance." *Id.* at 349, 713 S.E.2d at 286.

However, noncompliance with the recording requirement is excusable and is not alone a ground for dismissal (1) if the arresting officer submits a sworn affidavit certifying the video equipment was inoperable and stating which reasonable efforts were made to maintain it; (2) if the arresting officer submits a sworn affidavit that it was physically impossible to produce the videotape because either (a) the defendant needed emergency medical treatment or (b) exigent circumstances existed; (3) when an arrest is made and the camera has not been activated if video recording begins and conforms with the requirements as soon as practicable in circumstances including, but not limited to, road blocks, traffic accident investigations, and citizens' arrests; or (4) for any other valid reason for the failure to produce the video tape based upon the totality of the circumstances. § 56–5–2953(B).

Both the circuit court and the magistrate court committed errors of law by holding the statute required dismissal unless the video **77 recorded all of Taylor's actions. The statute's language is plain, unambiguous, and conveys a clear meaning, and consequently, the rules of statutory interpretation are unnecessary. Furthermore, the circuit court erred in making factual findings because it was sitting in an appellate capacity. *Rogers v. State,* 358 S.C. 266, 270, 594 S.E.2d 278, 280 (Ct.App.2004).

*305 *Suchenski, Murphy*, and *Gordon* demonstrate the plain language of the statute does not require the video to encompass every action of the defendant, but requires video of each event listed in the statute. Significantly, in each of these cases, the propriety of dismissal of the charges depended on whether the officer complied with the mandatory provisions of the statute. In *Suchenski,* although the court did not discuss the nature of the City's violation of the statute because the City conceded its noncompliance, the video stopped recording *before* the defendant was arrested. 374 S.C. at 14–15, 646 S.E.2d at 879–80; *see also* § 56–5–2953(A)(1)(a) (2006) (requiring video to "conclude *after* the arrest of the person for a violation of" a DUI offense (emphasis added)). In *Murphy*, the court found the officer complied with the statute even though the camera only recorded portions of the defendant's body during the sobriety tests because the prior statute did not specifically require video of sobriety tests. 392 S.C. at 628, 631–32, 709 S.E.2d at 686, 688. Additionally, the court noted the defendant did not allege the video did not record the officer giving *Miranda* warnings, which was required by the statute. *Id.* at 631, 709 S.E.2d at 688. Finally, in *Gordon,* after affirming the circuit court's determination that the statute required video recording of the HGN sobriety test, this court remanded to the magistrate court to determine whether the video captured the defendant's head during administration of the HGN test. 408 S.C. at 543–44, 759 S.E.2d at 758–59. This court noted the statutory provision requiring video recording of field sobriety tests administered is pointless "if the actual tests cannot be seen on the recording." *Id.* at 543, 759 S.E.2d at 758; *see also State v. Henkel,* 404 S.C. 626, 632, 746 S.E.2d 347, 351 (Ct.App.2013) (*cert. granted* ) (finding trial court erred in not dismissing the charge when officer failed to videotape the issuing of *Miranda* warnings and no exception applied).

The purpose of the video requirement in the statute "is to create direct evidence of a DUI arrest." *Town of Mt. Pleasant,* 393 S.C. at 347, 713 S.E.2d at 285. In enacting the provision, the legislature indicated this purpose and intent by specifically requiring the video to "include any field sobriety tests administered," as they determine whether a driver is impaired and therefore create direct evidence of the DUI *306 arrest. § 56–5–2953(A)(1)(a)(ii). In addition, unlike requiring the video to encompass every action of the defendant, requiring video recording of the person's arrest and of the officer issuing *Miranda* warnings serves to protect important rights of the defendant. However, this does not mean the legislature intended only those events enumerated in the statute to be recorded. The plain language of the statute demonstrates the legislature intended video recording of the majority of an officer's encounter with a potential DUI suspect. Nonetheless, interpreting the statute to require dismissal of the charges when the defendant is off camera for a short period of time and the gap does not occur during any of those events that either create direct evidence of a DUI or serve important rights of the defendant would result in an absurdity that could not possibly have been intended by the legislature. Indeed, interpreting the statute in that way would require dismissal of a DUI charge when a suspect stumbles out of view of the camera or when the officer is placing a suspect into his vehicle. Accordingly, section 56–5–2953 does not require dismissal of a DUI charge when the video recording of the incident briefly omits the suspect but that omission does not occur during any of those events that either create direct evidence of a DUI or serve important rights of the defendant.

Because the statute was not violated in this situation, submitting an affidavit was unnecessary. Moreover, affidavits are required only when the camera was inoperable or it was physically impossible to record because the defendant required emergency medical treatment or exigent circumstances existed. § 56–5–2953(B). The record contains **78** no evidence those situations were present here. As a result, the State did not need to submit an affidavit.

Although the video omitted Taylor from its view during the repositioning of Tolley's patrol vehicle, none of the field sobriety tests administered and none of the other statutory requirements occurred while she was out of the camera's view.

Because both the magistrate court and circuit court erred in interpreting the statute to require dismissal here, we reverse and remand to the magistrate court for trial.

**REVERSED AND REMANDED.**

HUFF and SHORT, JJ., concur.

Footnotes

[1]  The statute became effective February 10, 2009.

[2]  This statute also became effective February 10, 2009.

[3]      The magistrate's return is unclear whether the magistrate court reviewed the video. The return states "both parties agree that there is a gap on the video recording where the defendant is not on camera and her conduct is not being recorded," but does not state that the court watched the video. Additionally, neither the State nor Taylor offered any items into evidence before the magistrate court.

[4]      *Miranda v. Arizona,* 384 U.S. 436, 86 S.Ct. 1602, 16 L.Ed.2d 694 (1966).

[5]      It is also unclear whether the circuit court reviewed the video or made its findings based on statements by counsel during the hearing. Again, neither the State nor Taylor offered any items into evidence before the magistrate court. Nonetheless, Taylor has not challenged that the other requirements of the statute were met. Taylor only argued her omission from the camera's view for a period of time violated the statute because her conduct was not recorded.

[6]      Tolley charged Taylor with violating section 56–5–2933.

[7]      "Nystagmus is described as an involuntary jerking of the eyeball, a condition that may be aggravated by the effect of chemical depressants on the central nervous system." *State v. Sullivan,* 310 S.C. 311, 315 n. 2, 426 S.E.2d 766, 769 n. 2 (1993). "The HGN test consists of the driver being asked to cover one eye and focus the other on an object held at the driver's eye level by the officer. As the officer moves the object gradually out of the driver's field of vision toward his ear, he watches the driver's eyeballs to detect involuntary jerking." *Id.*

[8]      "In the walk and turn test, the subject is directed to take nine steps, heel-to-toe, along a straight line. After taking the steps, the suspect must turn on one foot and return in the same manner in the opposite direction. The examiner looks for eight indicators of impairment: if the suspect cannot keep balance while listening to the instructions, begins before the instructions are finished, stops while walking to regain balance, does not touch heel-to-toe, steps off the line, uses arms to balance, makes an improper turn, or takes an incorrect number of steps." *Appendix A: Standardized Field Sobriety Testing,* National Highway Traffic Safety Administration, at http://www.nhtsa.gov/people/injury/alcohol/sfst/appendix_a.htm (last visited Oct. 24, 2014).

[9]   Moreover, the *Murphy* court noted the legislature's amendment to the statute in 2009 bolstered its conclusion the previous statute was not violated when the video did not capture the defendant's performance on all of the field sobriety tests administered. 392 S.C. at 632 n. 4, 709 S.E.2d 685 at 688 n. 4.

# <u>SLED Regulations</u>

## Table of Contents
8.12.1 Breath Alcohol Device
8.12.2 Wet Bath Simulator
8.12.3 Breath Test Sites
8.12.4 Operator Certification
8.12.5 Administration of Breath Alcohol Tests
8.12.6 Datamaster DMT Status Code Messages and Inspections
8.12.7 Breath Site Video Recording Approval

## 8.12.1 BREATH ALCOHOL DEVICE

**GENERAL PURPOSE**: To set forth policies for the administration of implied consent breath alcohol tests.

**POLICY:** The Division will approve, certify, and inspect breath alcohol devices for the implied consent program.

**SPECIFIC PROCEDURES:**

A. APPROVAL

1. Alcohol, when mentioned in this document, refers to ethanol. The Division is statutorily responsible for approving breath alcohol devices, operators, and procedures by the authority of the implied consent laws and regulations of the State of South Carolina.

2. The DataMaster DMT (also known as the DataMaster) is the only evidential breath alcohol device approved by the Division. The current manufacturer is National Patent Analytical Systems, Inc., which is owned by Intoximeters, Inc. The DataMaster

DMT will remain approved even if the manufacturer changes. The DataMaster DMT has been tested and approved by the National Highway Traffic Safety Administration.

3. The DataMaster DMT is a breath alcohol device that performs an accurate chemical test to determine a subject's alcohol concentration (State vs. Squires, 426, SE 2nd 738, 1992). This instrument utilizes infrared spectroscopy to perform a chemical analysis of the breath. The chemistry of alcohol determines its infrared absorption characteristics. Chemicals, such as alcohol, absorb infrared light in specific amounts at specific wavelengths. The DataMaster DMT uses three infrared wavelengths to distinguish ethanol from any other possible substances.

## B. INITIAL INSPECTIONS

1. Each DataMaster DMT will pass an initial inspection by a SLED certified breath test specialist before instrument certification. This inspection is in addition to any manufacturer inspection and does not need repeating as long as the instrument is certified.

2. The following listed procedures occur during an initial inspection:

a. Visual inspection for correct software signature.

b. Confirmation of passwords to ensure proper access.

c. Identification of printed circuit boards.

d. Inspection of breath tube and rear panel connection.

e. Examination of check valves.

f. Inspection of inlet/outlet hoses for simulator connections.

g. Verification of simulator temperature.

h. Confirmation of instrument voltages

i. Confirmation of one and one-half liters volume requirement.

j. Verification of date and time.

k. Remote access of instrument using modem and phone line or internet connection.

l. Inspection of Breath Alcohol Analysis Test Report/Evidence ticket printout.

m. Calibration using a 0.08% alcohol concentration standard.

n. Performance of Linearity checks using at least three different alcohol concentrations.

C. CERTIFICATION

1. A SLED certified breath testing specialist will certify each DataMaster DMT. To obtain certification, an instrument will pass a calibration (establishment of calibration factors), a supervisor (a series of a minimum of five 0.08% alcohol concentration simulator tests), and diagnostic test (an internal diagnostic routine) at its site. If a testing site is a mobile van, the instrument remains certified regardless of the physical location of the van.

2. To pass the calibration and diagnostic test, no errors or failures may appear. To pass the supervisor test, the average simulator solution reading will be a 0.08% alcohol concentration (0.076% through 0.084%, inclusive), and the simulator solution temperature will be 34 degrees Celsius (C), 33.5 through 34.5, inclusive.

3. A certification record documenting the serial number, site location, date/time of certification, and identification of the SLED certified breath testing specialist will be completed. The certification record is also the documentation that the instrument passed the initial inspection. This information is maintained electronically for a minimum of five years.

4. A certification does not expire unless revoked by SLED. A new certification will be issued for each new site except when the instrument is moved to SLED or manufacturer's service center for repair, inspection, or storage and later moved back to its original site. In this case, an inspection is issued when the instrument is returned to its original site.

5. The certification record denotes the site where the instrument is certified for operation. The instrument may not be moved from this general location without SLED performing another site inspection. Movement of the instrument within a limited area, such as different locations within a room, may be done by the local agency without another site inspection or instrument certification by SLED.

6. The certification does not have to be repeated if the instrument or its software is upgraded. SLED will approve upgrades to the instrument or software before installation. Upgrades will be phased in, unless an urgent need exists.

7. Notification of significant upgrades to the instrument, as determined by the manufacturer, will be sent to the National Highway Traffic Safety Administration for evaluation and possible testing.

8. Certified breath testing devices at certified breath testing sites shall be utilized for their intended purpose of breath testing individuals who have been arrested for any of the offenses pertaining to the Implied Consent Laws of South Carolina, other alcohol related offenses, or for any other law enforcement purposes.

## 8.12.2 WET BATH SIMULATOR
**GENERAL PURPOSE:** To set forth policies for the administration of implied consent breath alcohol tests.
**POLICY:** The Division will approve and certify wet bath simulator devices to be used during every breath test in the calibration check process.
**SPECIFIC PROCEDURES:**
A. APPROVAL/CERTIFICATION

1. The Model 3402C-2K is the only simulator approved by the Division for use with the DataMaster DMT. The current manufacturer is REPCO Marketing Inc. The 3402C-2K will remain approved even if the manufacturer were to change. The 3402C-2K has been tested and approved by the National Highway Traffic Safety Administration. Simulators may be changed as needed among DataMasters.

2. The alcoholic breath simulator is a specifically designed, constant temperature water and alcohol solution wet bath device. An electronic probe checks the solution temperature during the breath test process.

3. The simulator solution temperature will be 34 degrees Celsius (C), 33.5 through 34.5, inclusive, to pass each test. If the simulator solution temperature is in this range, the test passes and the actual temperature will be printed on the Breath Alcohol Analysis Test Report/Evidence Ticket. If the temperature is not within this range, the test is aborted.

B. SOLUTION ANALYSIS/CERTIFICATION

1. An independent laboratory will analyze each lot of simulator solution. Additionally, each lot will be analyzed by SLED. The specific methods used by the independent laboratory and SLED may vary depending on instrumentation, etc.

2. The basic elements of the SLED analysis are:

a. Analysis is performed on an automated head-space gas chromatography system.

b. An internal standard quantitation method is utilized.

c. The headspace gas chromatography system is calibrated using alcohol standards.

d. A minimum of 2 bottles of simulator solution of a particular lot is sampled. A minimum of 6 samples per bottle is used for analysis.

e. The average of the simulator solution readings from all bottles should be 0.0968% alcohol concentration +/- 5% of the reading (0.0919% through 0.1016%, inclusive). NOTE: This range of solution concentration when used in a calibrated simulator, operating at 34 degrees Celsius (C), 33.5 through 34.5, inclusive, will give a reading of 0.08% alcohol concentration (0.076% through 0.084%, inclusive).

3. Only SLED certified simulator solution may be used in the breath alcohol testing process. SLED will issue a certification record for each lot of approved solution. The certification is valid from 12:01 A.M. of the date listed on the certification sheet.

4. The analytical data of the solution samples, independent lab report, and SLED certification record will be maintained electronically for a minimum of five years from the date of certification.

5. Each bottle will have a lot number, bottle number, an integrity seal, and an expiration date. A bottle of simulator solution may not be used after its expiration date.

## C. SOLUTION CHANGE PROTOCOL

1. The DataMaster DMT requires a solution change after 100 simulator tests or 31 days, whichever comes first. The solution may be changed at any time before the mandatory change. When a mandatory change is indicated, the instrument will not leave the "Change Soln Now" status until an acceptable solution change has been completed. It is acceptable for the period between solution changes to exceed 31 days, since the instrument will not allow breath tests to occur until the solution is changed.

2. After 90 simulator tests or 26 days, whichever comes first, the instrument will display, "Change Soln Soon". This message will be displayed on the instrument until a solution change is performed or a mandatory change is required.

3. Only certified operators will change the solution. Operators will enter the new lot/bottle number and expiration date of the solution used in a change. This information will be saved electronically by the instrument and will be populated on the "Solution Information" screen and printed on every Breath Alcohol Analysis Test Report/Evidence Ticket until the next solution change.

4. Specific questions are prompted to document the solution change. After the simulator solution (external standard) reaches proper temperature, 34 degrees Celsius (C), 33.5 through 34.5, inclusive, the instrument performs five simulator tests. All readings from the five tests will be 0.076% through 0.084%, inclusive, which constitutes a 0.08% alcohol concentration reading according to policy. The standard deviation will be 0.003% or less.

5. If a failure to meet these standards occurs, a mandatory solution change is required. The entire procedure will be repeated with a different bottle of solution. A failed solution change does not indicate the certified solution lot and/or bottle was improper, only that the readings obtained were outside acceptable limits. The bottle is changed only so that the solution counter may be reset. The solutions are verified by an independent laboratory and SLED.

## 8.12.3 BREATH TEST SITES
**GENERAL PURPOSE:** To set forth policies for the administration of implied consent breath alcohol tests.
**POLICY:** The Division will establish eligibility criteria for breath alcohol testing sites.
**SPECIFIC PROCEDURES:**

## A. ELIGIBILITY

1. Based on available funding and need, SLED may purchase DataMaster DMTs for testing sites. Preference is given to sites that have a significant number of implied consent arrests, and an overnight adult detention facility, or sites in a county seat.

2. With the concurrence of SLED, other agencies may purchase DataMaster DMTs to be submitted for SLED certification.

## B. REQUIREMENTS

1. Each potential site for a certified DataMaster DMT is required to pass a site inspection by a SLED certified breath test specialist. The certification record issued for each instrument serves as documentation the site inspection is approved.

2. The room temperature should be typically maintained between 65 degrees and 80 degrees Fahrenheit. NOTE: Monitoring of the site temperature is not required. If variances in site temperature become extreme, the instrument will abort the test due to varied status code messages.

3. Each site, except SLED, will have one dedicated phone line. Certified DataMaster DMTs at SLED are only required to have access to a phone line. Multiple DataMaster DMTs at the same site may each have a separate phone line or may, at the discretion of SLED, operate from one phone line using distinctive ring capability.

4. The phone line(s) may not be used for any purpose not related to the DataMaster DMTs.

5. Each site will have a high-speed internet connection.

6. Each site will have access to a 110-volt (normal household current) electrical line. The receptacle will be properly grounded and will be compatible with a three-prong plug. There will not be excessive demand on this line from other equipment.

7. Each site will be located in a secure building or van that can be secured by a lock.

## 8.12.4 OPERATOR CERTIFICATION
**GENERAL PURPOSE:** To set forth policies for the administration of implied consent breath alcohol tests.
**POLICY:** The Division will assist the South Carolina Criminal Justice Academy with operator certification/recertification.
**SPECIFIC PROCEDURES:**
A. The South Carolina Criminal Justice Academy, in consultation with SLED, is responsible for establishing eligibility requirements for DataMaster DMT operator training.

B. The South Carolina Criminal Justice Academy provides training for DataMaster DMT operator certification and recertification pursuant to SLED policies.

C. The certification period begins at 12:01 A.M. on the certification date and ends at 11:59 P.M. on the expiration date. Operator recertification will be conducted every two years. Only certified operators may perform tests on certified DataMaster DMTs.

## 8.12.5 ADMINISTRATION OF BREATH ALCOHOL TEST
**GENERAL PURPOSE:** To set forth policies for the administration of implied consent breath alcohol tests.

**POLICY:** The Division will establish procedures for properly conducting implied consent and non-implied consent DataMaster DMT breath alcohol tests.

**SPECIFIC PROCEDURES:**

A. IMPLIED CONSENT TESTS

1. Any arresting and/or primary investigating officer may direct that a subject under arrest or detained for an implied consent related offense submit to a breath alcohol test.

2. Except for Flying Under the Influence (FUI), any officer (if a certified operator), including the arresting and/or primary investigating officer, may administer the breath test if the observation period is video recorded.

3. SLED approved methods do not require the breath test be administered within any particular time after the arrest. The test should be administered as soon as practicable without undue delay. However, statutory time requirements do exist for some implied consent offenses.

B. NON-IMPLIED CONSENT TESTS

1. A non-implied consent test is any breath test on a SLED certified instrument not performed under the authority of the implied consent laws of South Carolina.

2. After a high reading on an implied consent test, the operator may perform a non-implied consent test if he/she is concerned about the subject's health. A high reading is defined as any significant reading that gives the operator concern regarding the subject's welfare. This reading is typically 0.35% alcohol concentration or greater. The results of this second test should not be used for court purposes. The operator does not have to

wait to perform a second test before seeking medical attention for a subject.

3. To perform a non-implied consent test, the operator will activate the appropriate icon on the DataMaster DMT touch-screen labeled as "Non-Implied Consent."

4. During a non-implied consent test, only minimal test questions will be prompted. The operational protocol may be the same as in an implied consent test. If a non-implied consent test is performed,

the instrument will denote this type of test on the Breath Alcohol Analysis Test Report/Evidence Ticket.

## C. BREATH TEST SEQUENCE

1. The breath test sequence for an implied consent test encompasses the following events: video recording of the breath test (if applicable), advisement process (Implied Consent Rights, if applicable), checking of the mouth, data entry, observation period, operational protocol, and printout of the Breath Alcohol Analysis Test Report/Evidence Ticket. (The DataMaster DMT performs the start of the observation period/time-stamp function automatically; therefore, the operator no longer manually activates this function.) To ensure a proper test is administered, a test is considered complete only after the operational protocol has finished and the signature lines are printed on the Breath Alcohol Analysis Test Report/Evidence Ticket. (For a non-implied consent test, video recording of the breath test, advisement process, checking of the mouth, and observation period are not required. However, to ensure an accurate test, checking of the mouth and the observation period are recommended.) If a subject refuses at any time prior to or during

the observation period, a simulator test does not need to be performed to ensure the instrument is in proper working order at the time of the test. (State v. Jansen, 305 S.C. 320, 408 S.E.2d 235 1991.) In this event, the operational protocol will be considered complete once the officer answers, "Yes," to the question, "Subject Refused?" In the event of a refusal, no further steps in the operational protocol need to be completed in order for the test to be defined as a completed test.

2. If a statute requires a video recording of the breath test, the test operator will activate the video recording equipment, advise the subject they are being video recorded, and inform the subject verbally and in writing of their Implied Consent Rights. If a video recording is not required, the operator is only required to inform the subject verbally and in writing of their Implied Consent Rights.

3. It is recommended, but not required, that the advisement process occur before checking of the mouth and the start of the observation period, however, it is a requirement that the subject be advised of his/her applicable Implied Consent Rights prior to providing a breath sample. A typical order of events would be advisement process, checking of the mouth, and start of the observation period.

4. Checking of the mouth will occur before the start of the observation period. The observation period is initiated at the point the operator answers the question, "Subject's Mouth Checked?" (The time the observation period begins is electronically stored by the DMT.) This question should be answered with a "Yes" only after the operator has checked the mouth for any foreign material and/or removable dental work. However, if the observation period is initiated before checking

of the mouth, the operator will abort/cancel the test and begin a new breath test sequence.

5. The test operator will begin the testing protocol/data entry process by touching the DataMaster DMT screen and entering the password. After all questions have been answered and all data has been entered and reviewed, the instrument begins the operational protocol. If all steps pass in the operational protocol, the subject is requested to provide a sample. After sample collection, the instrument completes the final steps of the operational protocol and prints the Breath Alcohol Analysis Test Report/Evidence Ticket.

6. The test operator and the arresting officer should sign the completed Breath Alcohol Analysis Test Report/Evidence Ticket on any implied consent test or refusal. (It is not required that the "Subject Copy" be signed.) Unless the subject is unruly, he/she should be given the opportunity to sign the test Breath Alcohol Analysis Test Report/Evidence Ticket and receive a copy, regardless of whether it is a test or refusal. (It is not required that the subject be given a copy of aborted tests.) The DataMaster DMT will print two copies of the Breath Alcohol Analysis Test Report/Evidence Ticket, one (1) for the testing/arresting officer and the second (2) for the subject.(It is not required that the "Subject Copy" be signed.)

D. ADVISEMENT FORMS

1. SLED will provide rights advisement forms for implied consent tests. Based on the type of test selected to be run, the DataMaster DMT will print the applicable advisement forms utilizing a stand-alone printer. Advisement forms will be printed in a Standard English version, and some forms may include a Spanish version. In applicable circumstances, a Spanish version

may be used in lieu of or in addition to the English version. The DataMaster DMT will print two copies of the applicable advisement, one (1) for the testing/arresting officer and the second (2) for the subject. If additional advisement forms are needed, press the touch-screen icon "Additional Advisements" on the main menu screen.

2. SLED's "DRIVING UNDER THE INFLUENCE ADVISEMENT" is to be read to subjects given breath alcohol tests for Driving Under the Influence (DUI) violations. The "FELONY DRIVING UNDER THE INFLUENCE ADVISEMENT" is to be read to subjects given breath alcohol tests for Felony DUI violations.

3. SLED's "COMMERCIAL DRIVER'S LICENSE ADVISEMENT" is to be read to subjects given breath alcohol tests for Commercial Driver's License (CDL) violations. If a DUI or Felony DUI charge is also involved, that applicable advisement should also be read to the subject. However, if no DUI or Felony DUI charge is involved, only the CDL advisement should be read to the subject.

4. SLED's "ZERO TOLERANCE ADVISEMENT" is to be read to subjects given breath alcohol tests for zero tolerance violations. If a DUI or Felony DUI charge is involved, that applicable advisement should be read to the subject in lieu of the zero tolerance advisement. If no DUI or Felony DUI charge is involved, only the zero tolerance advisement should be read to the subject.

5. SLED's "BOATING UNDER THE INFLUENCE (BUI) ADVISEMENT" is to be read to subjects given breath alcohol tests for applicable Boating Under the Influence (BUI) violations.

6. SLED's "BUI INVOLVING DEATH, BODILY INJURY, OR PROPERTY DAMAGE ADVISEMENT" is to be read to subjects given breath alcohol tests for applicable BUI violations.

7. SLED's "FLYING UNDER THE INFLUENCE ADVISEMENT" is to be read to subjects given breath alcohol tests for Flying Under the Influence (FUI) violations.

8. SLED's "SHOOTING UNDER THE INFLUENCE ADVISEMENT" is to be read to subjects given breath alcohol tests for shooting under the influence violations.

E. ADVISEMENT PROCESS

1. The advisement process consists of the officer reading any applicable advisements and furnishing the subject a copy. The reading of any applicable rights advisements and furnishing the subject a copy should be completed as soon as practical after the subject arrives at the testing site. The advisement process will be completed before the subject is requested to blow into the instrument. (The DataMaster DMT automatically prints two copies of the applicable advisement of rights form. One copy will be the Operator/Officer's copy that will be signed by the Subject and the Operator/Officer. This copy should also have the date/time recorded by the Operator/Officer. The second copy will be labeled in bold, "**Subject Copy**". This should be given to or placed in close proximity to the subject for his/her perusal. Only the Operator/Officer's copy needs to be signed.)

2. Unless the subject is unruly, he/she should be given the opportunity to sign the testing/arresting officer's copy of the advisement form. The only advisement form that needs to be filled out and signed is the copy that is retained by the

testing/arresting officer. The subject needs to be furnished only a copy of the applicable advisement form.

3. The subject's signature signifies only that he/she received a copy of the form. When the subject is provided a copy of the form, the subject has been informed in writing of his/her rights whether or not he/she signs the testing/arresting officer's copy of the advisement form.

4. The subject may sign the advisement form after the test as long as he/she is provided a copy before being requested to blow into the instrument. A subject is provided a copy if a copy is either given to him/her or made available by placing in his/her proximity where he/she can read it.

5. Whether or not the subject signs the advisement form, he/she will be furnished with a copy or a copy left with his/her items at the detention facility or other applicable location.

F. REFUSAL

1. A subject may be removed from the testing site at any time after a refusal occurs. If a subject gives the test operator a refusal after the advisement process, the checking of the mouth and/or observation period may be waived.

2. In the event a refusal occurs during the observation period, this period may be terminated. The operator can terminate the observation period by pressing the touch-screen icon "Abort Observation" displayed on the screen during the observation period. If the "Abort Observation" icon is activated, the instrument will display the question "Did the subject refuse?" If the operator answers this question with a "Yes", the instrument

will print "REFUSED" by the subject sample on the Breath Alcohol Analysis Test Report/Evidence Ticket.

3. Regardless of the type of refusal, the operator will proceed with the applicable breath test sequence on the DataMaster DMT. If a subject refuses at any time prior to or during the observation period, a simulator test does not need to be performed to ensure the instrument is in proper working order at the time of the test. (State v. Jansen, 305 S.C. 320, 408 S.E.2d 235 1991.) In this event, the operational protocol will be considered complete once the officer answers, "Yes," to the question, "Subject Refused?" In the event of a refusal, no further steps in the operational protocol need to be completed in order for the test to be defined as a completed test. Unless unusual circumstances exist, all refusals should be entered into the DataMaster DMT. This action is done solely for documentary and statistical purposes, not to check the instrument.

4. A refusal to submit to a breath test can occur in any of the following ways:

a. The subject expresses a refusal to take the test after being advised of his/her implied consent rights.

b. The subject refuses to cooperate or interferes with the administration of the test.

c. The subject acts unruly while the test is being administered. This includes the entire process from the time the subject encounters the operator until the test is complete.

d. The subject delays the administration of the test. The test operator is not required to wait until an attorney or other individual arrives at the test site.

e. The subject does not cooperate in the checking of his/her mouth. This includes, but is not limited to, failure to open mouth, failure to accurately answer questions about foreign material and/or dental work, and failure to remove foreign material and/or removable dental work.

f. The subject ingests prohibited substances during the observation period. This prohibition includes smoking during the observation period.

g. The subject intentionally regurgitates or refuses to rinse out his/her mouth after unintentional regurgitation.

h. The subject refuses to answer or incorrectly answers biographical information required by the operator. The operator, may at his/her discretion, test a subject without complete biographical information, as long as the operator has sufficient information to identify the subject.

i. The subject does not attempt to blow, pretends to blow, or does not blow an adequate sample, as determined by the instrument. Any subject will be able to provide an adequate sample, as determined by the instrument.

j. The subject intentionally causes the instrument to have an error or failure.

## G. CHECKING OF THE SUBJECT'S MOUTH FOR FOREIGN MATERIAL

1. The operator will look inside the subject's mouth and/or ask the subject if he/she has any foreign material and/or removable dental work in his/her mouth.

2. Dental work (removable or permanent) is not considered foreign material. Even though the presence of dental work will not affect the breath test when a minimum twenty-minute observation period is utilized, any removable dental work discovered in the mouth will be removed as a precaution.

3. If any foreign material and/or dental work is discovered and removed, it is neither necessary nor required the mouth be rinsed out, as long as the observation period is used.

4. Any foreign material and/or removable dental work discovered in the mouth will be removed before the observation period begins. If foreign material and/or removable dental work discovered in the mouth is removed, it is not required the operator denote what foreign material was removed.

5. If a subject intentionally misleads an operator concerning any foreign material and/or removable dental work, the subject has forfeited his/her right to have it removed. Permanent dental work or dental work that is difficult to remove (such that a dentist is required to safely remove it) will be left in the mouth, because it will not affect breath test results when a minimum twenty-minute observation period is used.

## H. BREATH ALCOHOL ANALYSIS TEST REPORT/EVIDENCE TICKET

1. Utilizing a stand-alone printer, the DataMaster DMT will print the Breath Alcohol Analysis Test Report/Evidence Ticket on standard 8½" x 11" copy paper. A copy of every Breath Alcohol

Analysis Test Report/Evidence Ticket used in an implied consent test, including aborted tests, should be saved.

2. Whether or not the subject signs the Breath Alcohol Analysis Test Report/Evidence Ticket, he/she should be furnished with a copy or a copy left with his/her items at the detention facility. (The DataMaster DMT automatically prints two copies of the Breath Alcohol Analysis Test Report/Evidence Ticket. One copy will be the Officer's copy that will be signed by the Subject and the Officer. This copy should also have the date/time recorded by the Officer. The second copy will be labeled in bold, "**Subject Copy**". Only the Officer's copy needs to be signed.)

3. If extra copies of the Breath Alcohol Analysis Test Report/Evidence Ticket are needed, the operator may press the "Copy" icon on the DataMaster DMT screen. The instrument will print a copy of the last test performed.

I. OBSERVATION PERIOD START TIME

1. The time the observation period begins is electronically stored by the DMT. The DataMaster DMT will denote the beginning of the observation period on the Breath Alcohol Analysis Test Report/Evidence Ticket unless a refusal has already occurred. This time is captured by the DataMaster DMT based on the operator answering "Yes" to the question prompted by the instrument, "Subject's Mouth Checked?" This question should only be answered with a "Yes" after the operator has looked inside the subject's mouth and/or asked the subject if he/she has any foreign material and/or removable dental work in his/her mouth.

2. The DataMaster DMT will not denote the beginning of the observation period on the Breath Alcohol Analysis Test Report/Evidence Ticket if the question prompted by the instrument, "Subject's Mouth Checked?" is answered with "No," followed by answering the question "Subject Refused?" with a "Yes."

3. If the operator answers "Yes." to the question "Subject's Mouth Checked?" the instrument will capture this time as the start of the observation period and automatically lock-out the operator for a minimum of 20 minutes before allowing a breath sample to be given.

4. If the operator answers "No." to the question "Subject's Mouth Checked?" followed by answering the question "Subject Refused?" with a "Yes," the instrument will not capture or record a time for the start of the observation period and the instrument will skip the 20 minute observation period and will not allow a breath sample to be given. In the event of a refusal, a simulator test does not need to be performed to ensure the instrument is in proper working order at the time of the test. (State v. Jansen, 305 S.C. 320, 408 S.E.2d 235 1991.) In this event, the operational protocol will be considered complete once the officer answers, "Yes," to the question, "Subject Refused?" No further steps in the operational protocol need to be completed in order for the test to be defined as a completed test.

5. For breath testing purposes, the "official time" is the time recorded by the DataMaster DMT. This time is recorded on both the Breath Alcohol Analysis Test Report/Evidence Ticket and internal memory of the DataMaster DMT and is used to establish if the operator has followed proper protocol.

J. OBSERVATION PERIOD

1. The purpose of the observation period is to allow for the deprivation of mouth alcohol. While the DataMaster DMT has the capability to detect the presence of mouth alcohol and will abort the test if significant mouth alcohol is detected, an observation period of a minimum of twenty minutes will be used as a precaution.

2. The operator is not required to maintain eye contact with the subject, but the operator will monitor the subject to ensure no external liquids and/or solids are ingested before providing a breath sample.

3. The DataMaster DMT will automatically lock-out the operator for a minimum of 20 minutes before allowing a breath sample to be given. Except in refusals, there will be a minimum of twenty minutes between the observation start time and the time listed by the subject's sample on the Breath Analysis Test Report/Evidence Ticket.

4. The subject may not smoke during the observation period. If ingestion of prohibited substances or any other type of compromise of the observation period occurs and the operator proceeds with the test, he/she will abort the current observation period and restart the testing protocol over again. Check the mouth, and begin another observation period. The advisement of Implied Consent Rights would not have to be repeated. If the observation period must be restarted, the original Breath Alcohol Analysis Test Report/Evidence Ticket should be saved.

5. Merely belching during the observation period will not affect the test results and therefore the mouth does not have to be rinsed out or another observation period begun.

6. If a subject regurgitates significant (as determined by the operator) solid and/or liquid matter into the mouth during the observation period, the operator will have the subject rinse his/her mouth out with water, check the mouth and restart the testing protocol over again (unless a refusal occurs). If significant regurgitation that could affect the test went undetected by the operator, the instrument's mouth alcohol detection system should abort the test.

7. The operator can terminate the observation period by pressing the abort button displayed on the screen during the observation period. If the abort button is activated, the instrument will display the question "Subject Refused?" If the operator answers this question with a "No", the instrument will print "INCOMPLETE SUBJECT TEST" by the subject sample on the Breath Alcohol Analysis Test Report/Evidence Ticket. The operator can then restart the testing protocol over again. The

advisement of Implied Consent Rights would not have to be repeated. However, all other data entry would have to be repeated. If the observation period must be restarted, the original Breath Alcohol Analysis Test Report/Evidence Ticket should be saved.

## K. DATA ENTRY

1. For all displayed questions, except middle initials, the test operator is required to enter data. If an initial is not known or does not exist, press the enter tab to by-pass that particular data entry field.

2. Data entry errors or omissions will not affect the accuracy of the test results or invalidate the test; however, the data should be entered accurately for documentary and statistical reasons.

3. The instrument will not accept entries of the wrong format for that particular question or obvious errors. If a question, other than initials or date of birth, cannot be answered for whatever reason (unknown, not relevant to subject, etc.), "NA" (for non-applicable or not available) should be entered. For a date of birth that is unknown or unavailable, the operator should enter an arbitrary date of 01/01/1900. If an answer is too long to enter completely, the information should be entered to the extent possible.

4. After proper entry into the computerized database, data will not be changed. If an operator discovers that incorrect data was entered either by error or incorrect information supplied by the subject, he/she should make the proper notations in his/her records. SLED does not need to be notified.

5. The operator has approximately three minutes to choose a function or answer each question or the test will abort.

a. Using the keyboard, enter password to access DataMaster DMT. Press touch-screen icon "OK".

b. Main Menu gives operator ability to choose, by touch-screen activation, one of the following functions:

i. "RUN" – Operator can conduct a breath test.

ii. "Help/Information" – Operator can get a copy of helpful information about the running of a breath test.

iii. "Solution Change" – Operator can conduct a solution change.

iv. "Inquiry Complaint" – Operator can enter an inquiry/complaint about testing.

v. "Additional Forms" – Operator can print additional advisement forms.

vi. "Copy" – Operator can print a copy of last breath test.

vii. "Log Off" – Logs operator out of instrument.

c. If the "RUN" function is chosen, the next screen will display the types of breath tests available. Choose one of the following types of tests by touch-screen activation:

• "Driving Under the Influence"
• "Felony Driving Under the Influence"
• "Zero Tolerance" (Under 21)
• "Boating Under the Influence"
• "Felony Boating Under the Influence"
• "Commercial Driver's License" (CDL)
• "Shooting Under the Influence"
• "Flying Under the Influence"
• "Non-Implied Consent"

6. Once a type of breath test is selected, the following sequence of questions is prompted using a combination of touch-screen and keyboard activation:

a. "Is Video Activated?" – Press applicable touch-screen icon: "Yes" or "No"

i. If "Yes", the next screen prompts Officer to enter the video code (SLED ID) located on video monitor.

ii. If "No", then the DataMaster DMT will prompt the question, "Do you need Affidavit Failure to Produce?", if type breath test being run has a statutory requirement to be video recorded.

b. "Enter Video Code Below" – Using keyboard, enter the unique alpha numeric code (SLED ID) provided on the video monitor. If code is entered correctly, press "OK" using the touch-screen. If code is entered incorrectly, the DMT will prompt you to re-enter code by refreshing the screen.

c. "Print Video Code on Subject's Test Report?" – Press applicable touch-screen icon: "Yes" or "No"

i. If "Yes", a unique Subject ID and Subject Password will be generated and printed on the bottom of the Breath Alcohol Analysis Test Report/Evidence Ticket.

ii. If "No", the Subject ID and Subject Password will be printed only on the Officer's copy of the Breath Analysis Test Report/Evidence Ticket. The "Subject Copy" will have printed, "Contact officer for video code information."

d. Two copies of the applicable "Advisement of Implied Consent Rights" form will be printed at this time. One copy will be the Officer's copy that will be signed by the Subject and the Officer. This copy should also have the date/time recorded by the Officer. The second copy will be labeled in bold, "**Subject Copy**". This should be given to the subject for his/her perusal. Only the Officer's copy needs to be signed.

e. "Advisement Form Printed?" – Press applicable touch-screen icon: "Yes" or "No"

f. "Subject Advised of Video Recording?" – This question will be asked only if Officer answers "Yes" to question, "Is Video Activated?" This question can only be answered with a "Yes."

g. "Subject Advised that a Breath Sample is being Requested?" – This question can only be answered with a "Yes."

h. "Subject Advised of Applicable Rights?" – This question can only be answered with a "Yes."

i. "Subject's Mouth Checked?" – Press applicable touch-screen icon: "Yes" or "No"

i. If "Yes", the DataMaster DMT will record this time as the start of the observation period and proceed to the next question.

ii. If "No", the DataMaster DMT prompts the question, "Subject Refused?"

j. "Scan Driver's License?" – Press applicable touch-screen icon: "Yes" or "No"

k. "Insert License into slot and hit OK."

l. "Subject Information" Screen asks for the following information to be entered utilizing the keyboard:

• Subject Name (F/M/L)
• Street/Apt/Box
• City/Town
• State
• Zip Code
• Date of Birth
• Race (drop down box provided)

- Sex (drop down box provided)
- License Number

- State Licensed (two letter state abbreviation)

Press applicable touch-screen icon: "Cancel" or "Next>"
m. "Arrest Information" Screen asks for the following
information to be entered utilizing the keyboard:

- Arresting Officer Name (F/M/L)
- County Code of Arrest (drop down box provided)
- Agency ORI #
- Traffic Ticket #, Citation # or Agency Case #
- Accident Involved? (drop down box provided)
- # of Injuries
- Arrest Date
- Arrest Time (24-Hour)

Press applicable touch-screen icon: "<Prev", "Cancel", or
"Next>"
n. "Operator Information" and "Solution Information" Screen
asks for the following information to be entered utilizing the
keyboard:

Operator Information
- Operator Name (F/M/L)
- Certification #
- Agency ORI #

Solution Information
- Lot #
- Bottle#
- Expiration Date

NOTE: This information is automatically populated from data entered during last solution change.

Press applicable touch-screen icon: "<Prev", "Cancel", or "Next>"

o. "Verify Data" Screen asks the following question: "Would you like to review the data that you have entered?" The operator must press the "Yes" icon in order to continue. The operator will then have the ability to check all information entered for accuracy. Corrections to data entry would be made at this time. After each screen is reviewed press the touch-screen icon "Next>" to scroll to next page.

p. "Subject Test: Observation Period" Screen – During this screen, the mandatory 20 minute observation period is being counted down by the DataMaster DMT. The "Status Box", indicating minutes/seconds remaining, appears in the lower left-hand corner of the screen. The "Abort Observation" icon is located in the upper right-hand corner of the screen. The "Abort Observation" icon is available in refusals situations and other exigent circumstances in which the observation period needs to be terminated.

If the "Abort Observation" icon is pressed, the DMT will prompt the question, "Did the subject refuse?" Press the touch-screen icon: "Yes" or "No" to proceed.

i. If "Yes." is pressed, the observation period is aborted and the operational protocol is completed. "SUBJECT REFUSED" is printed by "SUBJECT SAMPLE" on Breath Alcohol Analysis Test Report/Evidence Ticket. This is considered a completed test and signature lines will be printed on the Breath Alcohol Analysis Test Report/Evidence Ticket.

ii. If "No." is pressed, the result is an "INCOMPLETE SUBJECT TEST" which is printed on the Breath Alcohol

Analysis Test Report/Evidence Ticket. This is not a completed test and no signature lines will be printed.

L. OPERATIONAL PROTOCOL

1. The DataMaster DMT operational protocol consists of the following steps in this order:

a. PURGING
b. AMBIENT ZEROING
c. BLANK TEST
d. INTERNAL STANDARD
e. EXTERNAL STANDARD
f. PURGING
g. AMBIENT ZEROING
h. BLANK TEST
i. PLEASE BLOW
j. PURGING
k. BLANK TEST
l. INTERNAL STANDARD

2. These steps are defined as follows:

a. PURGING - Flushes sample chamber with room air.

b. AMBIENT ZEROING - Establishes a reference point for measurements. The test will abort if significant alcohol and/or interference are present in the room air and/or sample chamber.

c. BLANK TEST - A test to ensure no significant alcohol and/or interference is present in the room air and/or sample chamber. The test will abort if significant alcohol and/or interference are present.

d. INTERNAL STANDARD - A check of optical and electronic accuracy by using a quartz plate of known infrared absorption.

e. EXTERNAL STANDARD (0.08% SIMULATOR) - A reading of 0.076% through 0.084%, inclusive, constitutes a 0.08% alcohol concentration reading according to SLED policy and passes test. Any reading outside this range constitutes a failure and the test aborts. The external standard (simulator) test serves as a calibration check for the system and shows whether the instrument is functioning properly (along with the other checks).

f. PLEASE BLOW - The instrument will display, "PLEASE BLOW", at the time for the subject to blow. The test operator will ensure a new mouthpiece is placed on the breath tube, unless a refusal has already occurred. The subject may use the same mouthpiece in the event the test is aborted and must be started again. The subject is given approximately two minutes to provide an acceptable breath sample.

i. The subject will provide a continuous breath sample, acceptable to the instrument, containing a minimum of approximately one and one half liters. "PLEASE BLOW" will display until an adequate sample is obtained or time expires.

ii. The instrument will indicate if the subject has significant mouth alcohol on his/her breath. Belching during the process of providing a breath sample will have no effect on the breath test reading.

iii. Regurgitating during the process of providing a breath sample, to an extent that would affect the test results, would cause the instrument to abort the test.

iv. An "INVALID SAMPLE DETECTED" or "DETECTOR OVERFLOW DETECTED" reading is not a completed test. Additionally, an "INVALID SAMPLE DETECTED" or "DETECTOR OVERFLOW DETECTED" reading, by itself, is not a refusal situation. If an "INVALID SAMPLE DETECTED" or "DETECTOR OVERFLOW DETECTED" reading is obtained and the arresting officer still desires a breath test, the checking of the mouth and the start of a new observation period are required to be repeated. However, the advisement process is not required to be repeated.

v. The instrument will indicate if significant interference is present in the subject's breath. In this case, the breath sample is not acceptable, and the instrument will display "INTERFERENCE DETECTED".

vi. An "INTERFERENCE DETECTED" reading is not a completed test and, by itself, is not a refusal situation. If necessary, medical attention should be given to the subject. The operator may elect to continue to administer a breath test. In this case, the advisement process, checking of the mouth, and observation period are not required to be repeated.

vii. If an acceptable breath sample is not provided in two minutes, the instrument will display "Did the subject refuse?" When question is prompted, press the touch-screen icon, "Yes" or "No." If "Yes" is answered, the instrument will print "REFUSED" by "SUBJECT SAMPLE", after the final steps of the operational protocol are completed. This is considered a completed test and signature lines will be printed on the Breath Alcohol Analysis Test Report/Evidence Ticket. If "No" is answered, the test will abort and the instrument will print "INCOMPLETE SUBJECT TEST" on the Breath Alcohol Analysis Test Report/Evidence Ticket. An "INCOMPLETE

SUBJECT TEST" reading, by itself, is not a refusal situation. (A "NO" should only be entered if the subject failed to provide an acceptable breath sample through no fault of his/her own.) In the event of an "INCOMPLETE SUBJECT TEST", the breath test sequence may be repeated, except the advisement process is not required to be repeated. This is not a completed test and no signature lines will be printed.

## M. BREATH ALCOHOL ANALYSIS TEST REPORT/EVIDENCE TICKET PRINTOUT

1. The start of the observation period and instrument serial number will be printed on the Breath Alcohol Analysis Breath Report/Evidence Ticket. With the exception of accident and injury data, all other entered biographical data will be printed on the Breath Alcohol Analysis Test Report/Evidence Ticket. If applicable and per Officer discretion, Subject ID and Subject Password will be printed at the bottom of the Breath Alcohol Analysis Test Report/Evidence Ticket, which is used to access the breath test video recording. Simulator test results will be displayed in thousandths of a percent. Blank tests and subject test results will be truncated and displayed in hundredths of a percent.

2. Alcohol concentration is used for reporting results of breath alcohol tests. Alcohol concentration is the number of grams of alcohol for each two hundred and ten liters of breath by weight (pursuant to Section 56-1-10, S.C. Code of Laws, 1976, as amended for breath, a bodily fluid other than blood). The forensically and medically accepted alveolar air to blood conversion factor of 2100 to 1 is used in converting breath alcohol measurements to blood alcohol measurements. This ratio means that 1 milliliter of blood contains approximately the same amount of alcohol as 2100 milliliters of alveolar air.

# 8.12.6 DATAMASTER DMT STATUS CODE MESSAGES AND INSPECTIONS

**GENERAL PURPOSE:** To set forth policies for the administration of implied consent breath alcohol tests.

**POLICY:** The Division will establish procedures for properly conducting implied consent DataMaster DMT breath alcohol tests.

**SPECIFIC PROCEDURES:**

A. STATUS CODE MESSAGES

1. Any status code message occurring during the operational protocol will cause the test to abort. The instrument is programmed to eliminate any chance of an improper test. All checks, such as internal standard, simulator solution temperature, simulator solution reading, etc., will pass or the test is aborted at the point of the failed check. All status codes are electronically recorded by the DataMaster DMT.

2. A simulator test, two internal standard tests, and other operational protocol steps inspect the instrument each time a subject test is performed. This inspection ensures the instrument is working properly with every subject test, regardless of any prior or subsequent status code messages. Previous or subsequent status code messages do not affect the accuracy of a completed test.

3. If the officer transports the subject to another breath testing site because of equipment or other issues, the officer will re-initiate the breath testing sequence. If necessary to comply with statutory requirements related to breath site video recording, the advisement process should be repeated at the new site.

4. If a subject provides an acceptable breath sample and the test is aborted before completion, the subject may be required to provide another sample since aborted tests are not considered completed tests. If the test is aborted, the operational protocol should be repeated. The advisement process, checking of the mouth, and observation period do not have to be repeated unless required by specific policy.

5. An aborted test is not considered a second breath test because a test has not been completed. If a reading is obtained for the subject sample, but a status code message then occurs and aborts the test, this test is not a valid or completed test, and the test should be repeated. The test may be repeated on either the same instrument or another instrument. If the same status code message were to occur again on the same instrument, it would again abort the test. The test operator should retain copies of all aborted tests.

6. If a status code message of "EXTERNAL STANDARD OUT OF RANGE" (0.08% simulator test) is encountered during a subject test, this condition does not indicate the simulator solution (lot or bottle) or calibration is improper. This status code message ("EXTERNAL STANDARD OUT OF RANGE") only indicates that the calibration check did not pass. It is not required or even suggested the bottle of simulator solution be changed or the instrument be recalibrated after one or more "EXTERNAL STANDARD OUT OF RANGE" status code message(s). The purpose of the simulator test is to verify the performance of the entire instrumental system, not the accuracy of the solution lot/bottle or calibration. Before field usage, the solutions are verified by an independent laboratory and SLED.

B. INSPECTIONS AFTER CERTIFICATION

1. A SLED certified breath test specialist will begin an inspection on every certified breath alcohol device (either remotely, via computer modem/internet connection, or on-site) at least once every three months and issue a SLED inspection report upon completion.

2. The inspection may begin before three months has elapsed and not be completed until after the three-month period. Therefore, the time lapse between inspection reports may exceed three months.

3. No instrument may be removed from its assigned site by an agency other than SLED without receiving approval from the SLED Implied Consent Department.

4. Status code messages do not require an inspection or repair action to be undertaken. When a status code message repeatedly occurs, an inspection and/or repair may be performed. A SLED certified breath test specialist and/or manufacturer's service representative will perform all repairs of breath alcohol devices.

5. Any inspection will have at least a supervisor test (a series of a minimum of five 0.08% alcohol concentration simulator tests) or diagnostic test (an internal diagnostic routine). A supervisor and/or diagnostic test may be performed without the completion of an inspection record. To pass the supervisor test, the simulator solution average reading will be a 0.08% alcohol concentration (0.076% through 0.084%, inclusive), and the simulator solution temperature will be 34 degrees Celsius (C), 33.5 through 34.5, inclusive. To pass the diagnostic test, no errors or failures may appear.

6. After a repair is completed, a SLED certified breath test specialist and/or manufacturer's service representative will

inspect the instrument before it is placed back into service and issue an inspection record. However, inspections not involving repair action may be performed remotely.

7. After an inspection, an inspection record, with serial number, site location, date/time of completion, and name of SLED certified breath testing specialist and/or manufacturer's service representative will be completed documenting the instrument is working properly. Inspection

records do not require the signature of the SLED certified breath testing specialist and/or manufacturer's service representative, since the name is listed on the report. These records are maintained electronically for a minimum of five years.

8. Upgrades, deemed significant by SLED, will be added to the inspection record. No other documentation of upgrades or their approval is required.

9. Recalibrations are done when necessary, with this action denoted on the inspection record. Since calibration checks are performed during each test, no specific interval exists at which an instrument will be recalibrated.

10. Three calibration checks (simulator test and two internal standards) are performed with each subject test. A failed calibration check does not necessarily require recalibration, but repeated failed calibration checks may require an inspection, repair, and/or recalibration.

11. The DataMaster DMT will electronically record and save for uploading to SLED's website status codes, inspections, maintenance/repairs, malfunctions, inquiries/complaints, and all breath test data. Records will be automatically recorded by the

DataMaster DMT. The DataMaster DMT provides the ability for the Operator/Officer to electronically enter any and all remarks by pressing the touch-screen icon "Inquiries/Complaints" located on the main menu screen. Retrieved data will be maintained electronically for a minimum of five years. However, the accidental/unavoidable loss of data does not invalidate any tests.

C. VERIFICATION OF LINEARITY

1. A SLED certified breath test specialist or a service representative of the instrument's manufacturer will perform a Linearity Verification on every certified breath alcohol device at least once a year.

2. Linearity Verification will consist of a series of five simulator tests performed at three different levels of concentration of simulator solution.

3. Linearity Verification records will be posted under Verification of Linearity on SLED's Implied Consent website.

# 8.12.7 BREATH SITE VIDEO RECORDING
**GENERAL PURPOSE:** To set forth policies for breath site video recording.
**POLICY:** The Division will approve and certify video recording systems for breath sites.
**SPECIFIC PROCEDURES:**
A. SYSTEM APPROVAL/CERTIFICATION

1. SLED will approve such methods for performing video recordings, at breath testing sites, that are demonstrated to the satisfaction of SLED to produce quality and reliable reproductions. The only approved video recording system is the

IRSA Video Recording System, IRSA Video and The W. H. Platts Company. This system was previously known as The W.H. Platts Company's VDS-2...

2. A SLED certified video recording specialist will certify each IRSAVideo Recording System. For a video recording system whose testing station is a mobile van, once the video recording system is certified for use in the van, it remains certified regardless of the physical location of the van.

3. A certification record documenting the serial number, site location, date/time, and name of SLED certified video recording specialist will be completed and maintained by SLED. A record will be issued for each new site except when the system is moved to SLED or manufacturer's service representative for inspection, repair, maintenance, or storage and later moved back to its original site. Certification records do not require the signature of the SLED video recording specialist, since the name is listed on the report. These records are maintained electronically by SLED for a minimum of five years.

4. A new certification is not required if a system component(s) is replaced, but is required if the entire system is replaced. A certification does not expire unless revoked by SLED.

B. SYSTEM INSPECTIONS

1. SLED certified video recording specialists and/or manufacturer's service representatives may inspect, repair, or maintain video recording systems. SLED will begin an on-site inspection on every certified VDS–2 at least once every twelve months and a report will be issued upon completion. The inspection may begin before twelve months has elapsed and not be completed until after the twelve-month period. Therefore, the

time lapse between inspection reports may exceed twelve months.

2. After an inspection, an inspection record, with serial number, site location, date/time of completion, and name of SLED certified video recording specialist will be completed documenting the system is

working properly. Inspection records do not require the signature of the SLED certified video recording specialist and/or manufacturer's service representative, since the name is listed on the report. These records are maintained electronically by SLED for a minimum of five years.

3. No system should be removed from its assigned site by an agency other than SLED and/or the manufacturer without first notifying the SLED Implied Consent Department and receiving approval.

## C. SYSTEM MISCELLANEOUS

1. No operator certification or forms are required to operate a SLED certified video recording system; therefore, any officer may operate this equipment. In addition, any officer may advise the subject of video recording.

2. The SLED video recording systems will produce a video recording of the breath test.

(a) The resulting subject's breath-test video recording will be treated with confidentiality.
(b) Therefore, in general, the subject's breath-test video recording, or access codes to the video recording, will be

released to third parties only with the authorization of the subject.

(c) However, due to the statutory requirements placed upon SLED as a government agency, release of a subject's breath-test video recording to third parties may occur under the following circumstances:

(i) When the requestor is an investigating police department or sheriff's office, and the third party is the responsible Solicitor's office.

(ii) When authorized by the responsible Solicitor's office and the requestor is an investigating police department or sheriff's office.

(iii)In response to valid subpoenas and court orders.

(iv)In response to valid requests made under the S.C. Freedom of Information Act.

3. The video recording systems may be used to comply with statutory requirements related to video recording. Additionally, these systems may be used to document breath tests not involving mandatory recording.

**APPROVAL**

| | | |
|---|---|---|
| Department Supervisor (Issuing Authority): Deborah H. Banks | _____ _____ _____ | Date: _____ _____ |
| Technical Leader: N/A | _____ _____ _____ | Date: _____ _____ |
| Quality Manager: Laurie J. Shacker | _____ _____ _____ | Date: _____ _____ |
| Captain: Wendy C. Bell, Ph.D. | _____ _____ _____ | Date: _____ _____ |
| Laboratory Director: C. Todd Hughey, Ph.D. | _____ _____ | Date: _____ (Effective Date) |

# Statute

## ARTICLE 23

*Reckless Homicide; Reckless Driving; Driving While Under the Influence of Intoxicating Liquor, Drugs or Narcotics*

**SECTION 56-5-2910. Reckless vehicular homicide; penalties; revocation of driver's license; reinstatement of license; conditions; consequences for subsequent violations.**

(A) When the death of a person ensues within three years as a proximate result of injury received by the driving of a vehicle in reckless disregard of the safety of others, the person operating the vehicle is guilty of reckless vehicular homicide. A person who is convicted of, pleads guilty to, or pleads nolo contendere to reckless vehicular homicide is guilty of a felony, and must be fined not less than one thousand dollars nor more than five thousand dollars or imprisoned not more than ten years, or both. The Department of Motor Vehicles shall revoke for five years the driver's license of a person convicted of reckless vehicular homicide.

(B) After one year from the date of revocation, the person may petition the circuit court in the county of the person's residence for reinstatement of the person's driver's license. The person shall serve a copy of the petition upon the solicitor of the county. The solicitor shall notify the representative of the victim of the reckless vehicular homicide of the person's intent to seek reinstatement of the person's driver's license. The solicitor or his designee within thirty days may respond to the petition and demand a hearing on the merits of the petition. If the solicitor or his designee does not demand a hearing, the circuit court shall consider any affidavit submitted by the petitioner and the solicitor or his designee when determining whether the conditions required for driving privilege reinstatement have been met by the petitioner. The court may order the reinstatement of the person's driver's license upon the following conditions:

(1) intoxicating alcohol, beer, wine, drugs, or narcotics were not involved in the vehicular accident which resulted in the reckless homicide conviction or plea;

(2) the petitioner has served the term of imprisonment or paid the fine, assessment, and restitution in full, or both; and

(3) the person's overall driving record, attitude, habits, character, and driving ability would make it safe to reinstate the privilege of operating a motor vehicle.

The circuit court may order the reinstatement of the driver's license before the completion of the full five-year revocation period, or the judge may order the granting of a route restricted license for the remainder of the five-year period to allow the person to drive to and from employment or school, or the judge may place other restrictions on the driver's license reinstatement. The order of the judge must be transmitted to the Department of Motor Vehicles within ten days.

(C) If the person's privilege to operate a motor vehicle is reinstated, a subsequent violation of the motor vehicle laws for any moving violation requires the automatic cancellation of the person's driver's license and imposition of the full period of revocation for the reckless vehicular homicide violation.


**SECTION 56-5-2920. Reckless driving; penalties; suspension of driver's license for second or subsequent offense.**

Any person who drives any vehicle in such a manner as to indicate either a wilful or wanton disregard for the safety of persons or property is guilty of reckless driving. The Department of Motor Vehicles, upon receiving satisfactory evidence of the conviction, of the entry of a plea of guilty or the forfeiture of bail of any person charged with a second and subsequent offense for the violation of this section shall forthwith suspend the driver's license of any such person for a period of three months. Only those offenses which occurred within a period of five years including and immediately preceding the date of the last offense shall constitute prior offenses within the meaning of this section. Any person violating the provisions of this section shall, upon conviction, entry of a plea of guilty or forfeiture of bail, be punished by a fine of not less than twenty-five dollars nor more than two hundred dollars or by imprisonment for not more than thirty days.

**SECTION 56-5-2930. Operating motor vehicle while under influence of alcohol or drugs; penalties; enrollment in Alcohol and Drug Safety Action Program; prosecution.**

(A) It is unlawful for a person to drive a motor vehicle within this State while under the influence of alcohol to the extent that the person's faculties to drive a motor vehicle are materially and appreciably impaired, under the influence of any other drug or a combination of other drugs or substances which cause impairment to the extent that the person's faculties to drive a motor vehicle are materially and appreciably impaired, or under the combined influence of alcohol and any other drug or drugs or substances which cause impairment to the extent that the person's faculties to drive a motor vehicle are materially and appreciably impaired. A person who violates the provisions of this section is guilty of the offense of driving under the influence and, upon conviction, entry of a plea of guilty or of nolo contendere, or forfeiture of bail must be punished as follows:

(1) for a first offense, by a fine of four hundred dollars or imprisonment for not less than forty-eight hours nor more than thirty days. However, in lieu of the forty-eight hour minimum imprisonment, the court may provide for forty-eight hours of public service employment. The minimum forty-eight hour imprisonment or public service employment must be served at a time when the person

is not working and does not interfere with his regular employment under terms and conditions the court considers proper. However, the court may not compel an offender to perform public service employment in lieu of the minimum forty-eight hour sentence. If the person's alcohol concentration is at least ten one-hundredths of one percent but less than sixteen one-hundredths of one percent, then the person must be punished by a fine of five hundred dollars or imprisonment for not less than seventy-two hours nor more than thirty days. However, in lieu of the seventy-two hour minimum imprisonment, the court may provide for seventy-two hours of public service employment. The minimum seventy-two hour imprisonment or public service employment must be served at a time when the person is not working and does not interfere with his regular employment under terms and conditions as the court considers proper. However, the court may not compel an offender to perform public service employment in lieu of the minimum sentence. If the person's alcohol concentration is sixteen one-hundredths of one percent or more, then the person must be punished by a fine of one thousand dollars or imprisonment for not less than thirty days nor more than ninety days. However, in lieu of the thirty-day minimum imprisonment, the court may provide for thirty days of public service employment. The minimum thirty days imprisonment or public service employment must be served at a time when the person is not working and does not interfere with his regular employment under terms and conditions as the court considers proper. However, the court may not compel an offender to perform public service employment instead of the thirty-day minimum sentence. Notwithstanding the provisions of Sections 22-3-540, 22-3-545, and 22-3-550, a first offense charged for this item may be tried in magistrates court;

(2) for a second offense, by a fine of not less than two thousand one hundred dollars nor more than five thousand one hundred dollars, and imprisonment for not less than five days nor more than one year. However, the fine imposed by this item must not be suspended in an amount less than one thousand one hundred dollars. If the person's alcohol concentration is at least ten one-hundredths of one percent but less than sixteen one-hundredths of one percent, then the person must

be punished by a fine of not less than two thousand five hundred dollars nor more than five thousand five hundred dollars and imprisonment for not less than thirty days nor more than two years. However, the fine imposed by this item must not be suspended in an amount less than one thousand one hundred dollars. If the person's alcohol concentration is sixteen one-hundredths of one percent or more, then the person must be punished by a fine of not less than three thousand five hundred dollars nor more than six thousand five hundred dollars and imprisonment for not less than ninety days nor more than three years. However, the fine imposed by this item must not be suspended in an amount less than one thousand one hundred dollars;

(3) for a third offense, by a fine of not less than three thousand eight hundred dollars nor more than six thousand three hundred dollars, and imprisonment for not less than sixty days nor more than three years. If the person's alcohol concentration is at least ten one-hundredths of one percent but less than sixteen one-hundredths of one percent, then the person must be punished by a fine of not less than five thousand dollars nor more than seven thousand five hundred dollars and imprisonment for not less than ninety days nor more than four years. If the person's alcohol concentration is sixteen one-hundredths of one percent or more, then the person must be punished by a fine of not less than seven thousand five hundred dollars nor more than ten thousand dollars and imprisonment for not less than six months nor more than five years; or

(4) for a fourth or subsequent offense, by imprisonment for not less than one year nor more than five years. If the person's alcohol concentration is at least ten one-hundredths of one percent but less than sixteen one-hundredths of one percent, then the person must be punished by imprisonment for not less than two years nor more than six years. If the person's alcohol concentration is sixteen one-hundredths of one percent or more, then the person must be punished by imprisonment for not less than three years nor more than seven years.

(B) No part of the minimum sentences provided in this section may be suspended. Instead of public service employment the court may invoke another sentence provided in this section. For a second or subsequent offense of this section, the service of the minimum sentence is mandatory. However, the judge may provide for the sentence to be served upon terms and conditions as he considers proper including, but not limited to, weekend service or nighttime service in any fashion he considers necessary.

(C) The fine for a first offense must not be suspended. The court is prohibited from suspending a monetary fine below that of the next preceding minimum monetary fine.

(D) For the purposes of this section, a conviction, entry of a plea of guilty or of nolo contendere, or forfeiture of bail for the violation of a law or ordinance of this or another state or a municipality of this or another state that prohibits a person from driving a motor vehicle while under the influence of intoxicating liquor, drugs, or narcotics, including, but not limited to, this section, or prohibits a person from driving a motor vehicle with an unlawful alcohol concentration, including, but not limited to, Section 56-5-2933, constitutes a prior offense of this section. Only those violations which occurred within a period of ten years including and immediately preceding the date of the last violation constitute prior violations within the meaning of this section.

(E) Upon imposition of a sentence of public service, the defendant may apply to the court to be allowed to perform his public service in his county of residence if he has been sentenced to public service in a county where he does not reside.

(F) One hundred dollars of each fine imposed pursuant to this section must be placed by the Comptroller General into a special restricted account to be used by the Department of Public Safety for the Highway Patrol.

(G) Two hundred dollars of the fine imposed pursuant to subsection

(A)(3) must be placed by the Comptroller General into a special restricted account to be used by the State Law Enforcement Division to offset the costs of administration of the breath testing devices, breath testing site video program, and toxicology laboratory.

(H) A person convicted of violating this section, whether for a first offense or subsequent offense, must enroll in and successfully complete an Alcohol and Drug Safety Action Program certified by the Department of Alcohol and Other Drug Abuse Services. An assessment of the extent and nature of the alcohol and drug abuse problem of the applicant must be prepared and a plan of education or treatment, or both, must be developed for the applicant. The Alcohol and Drug Safety Action Program shall determine if the applicant successfully has completed the services. The applicant must attend the first Alcohol and Drug Safety Action Program available after the date of enrollment. The Department of Alcohol and Other Drug Abuse Services shall determine the cost of services provided by each certified Alcohol and Drug Safety Action Program. Each applicant shall bear the cost of services recommended in the applicant's plan of education or treatment. The cost may not exceed five hundred dollars for education services, two thousand dollars for treatment services, and two thousand five hundred dollars in total for all services. An applicant may not be denied services due to an inability to pay. Inability to pay for services may not be used as a factor in determining if the applicant has successfully completed services. An applicant who is unable to pay for services shall perform fifty hours of community service as arranged by the Alcohol and Drug Safety Action Program, which may use the completion of this community service as a factor in determining if the applicant successfully has completed services. The court must be notified whether an offender failed to enroll in a certified program within thirty days or failed to participate in the plan of education or treatment. The court may hold the individual in contempt of court if the individual cannot show cause as to why no enrollment occurred within the mandated thirty days or why no progress has been made on the plan of education or treatment.

(I) A person charged for a violation of this section may be prosecuted

140

pursuant to Section 56-5-2933 if the original testing of the person's breath or collection of other bodily fluids was performed within two hours of the time of arrest and reasonable suspicion existed to justify the traffic stop. A person may not be prosecuted for both a violation of this section and a violation of Section 56-5-2933 for the same incident. A person who violates the provisions of this section is entitled to a jury trial and is afforded the right to challenge certain factors including the following:

(1) whether or not the person was lawfully arrested or detained;

(2) the period of time between arrest and testing;

(3) whether or not the person was given a written copy of and verbally informed of the rights enumerated in Section 56-5-2950;

(4) whether the person consented to taking a test pursuant to Section 56-5-2950, and whether the:

(a) reported alcohol concentration at the time of testing was eight one-hundredths of one percent or more;

(b) individual who administered the test or took samples was qualified pursuant to Section 56-5-2950;

(c) tests administered and samples obtained were conducted pursuant to Section 56-5-2950 and regulations adopted pursuant to Section 56-5-2951(O) and Section 56-5-2953(F); and

(d) machine was working properly.

(J) Nothing contained in this section prohibits the introduction of:

(1) the results of any additional tests of the person's breath or other bodily fluids;

(2) any evidence that may corroborate or question the validity of the

breath or bodily fluid test result including, but not limited to:

(a) evidence of field sobriety tests;

(b) evidence of the amount of alcohol consumed by the person; and

(c) evidence of the person's driving;

(3) a video recording of the person's conduct at the incident site and breath testing site taken pursuant to Section 56-5-2953 which is subject to redaction under the South Carolina Rules of Evidence; or

(4) any other evidence of the state of a person's faculties to drive a motor vehicle which would call into question the results of a breath or bodily fluid test.

At trial, a person charged with a violation of this section is allowed to present evidence relating to the factors enumerated above and the totality of the evidence produced at trial may be used by the jury to determine guilt or innocence. A person charged with a violation of this section must be given notice of intent to prosecute under the provisions of this section at least thirty calendar days before his trial date.

(K) For the purpose of this section, any offense carrying a penalty of imprisonment of ninety days or less may be tried in magistrates court.

(L) In cases in which enhanced penalties for higher levels of alcohol concentration may be applicable, upon the determination of guilt, the finder of fact shall determine the alcohol concentration and the judge shall apply the appropriate penalty. In cases involving jury trials, upon the return of a guilty verdict by the jury, the judge shall instruct the jury to make a finding of fact as to the following: "We the jury find the alcohol concentration of the defendant to be (1) at least eight one-hundredths of one percent but less than ten one-hundredths of one percent; (2) at least ten one-hundredths of one percent but less than sixteen one-hundredths of one percent; or (3) sixteen one hundredths

142

of one percent or more." Based on the jury's finding of fact, the judge shall apply the appropriate penalty. If the jury cannot reach a unanimous verdict as to the finding of fact, then the judge shall sentence the defendant based on the nonenhanced penalties.

**SECTION 56-5-2933. Driving with an unlawful alcohol concentration; penalties; enrollment in Alcohol and Drug Safety Action Program; prosecution.**

(A) It is unlawful for a person to drive a motor vehicle within this State while his alcohol concentration is eight one-hundredths of one percent or more. A person who violates the provisions of this section is guilty of the offense of driving with an unlawful alcohol concentration and, upon conviction, entry of a plea of guilty or of nolo contendere, or forfeiture of bail must be punished as follows:

(1) for a first offense, by a fine of four hundred dollars or imprisonment for not less than forty-eight hours nor more than thirty days. However, in lieu of the forty-eight hour minimum imprisonment, the court may provide for forty-eight hours of public service employment. The minimum forty-eight hour imprisonment or public service employment must be served at a time when the person is not working and does not interfere with his regular employment under terms and conditions the court considers proper. However, the court may not compel an offender to perform public service employment in lieu of the minimum forty-eight hour sentence. If the person's alcohol concentration is at least ten one-hundredths of one percent but less than sixteen one-hundredths of one percent, then the person must be punished by a fine of five hundred dollars or imprisonment for not less than seventy-two hours nor more than thirty days. However, in lieu of the seventy-two hour minimum imprisonment, the court may provide for seventy-two hours of public service employment. The minimum seventy-two hour imprisonment or public service employment must be served at a time when the person is not working and does not interfere with his regular employment under terms and conditions as the court considers proper.

However, the court may not compel an offender to perform public service employment in lieu of the minimum sentence. If the person's alcohol concentration is sixteen one-hundredths of one percent or more, then the person must be punished by a fine of one thousand dollars or imprisonment for not less than thirty days nor more than ninety days. However, in lieu of the thirty-day minimum imprisonment, the court may provide for thirty days of public service employment. The minimum thirty days imprisonment or public service employment must be served at a time when the person is not working and does not interfere with his regular employment under terms and conditions as the court considers proper. However, the court may not compel an offender to perform public service employment instead of the thirty-day minimum sentence. Notwithstanding the provisions of Sections 22-3-540, 22-3-545, and 22-3-550, a first offense charged for this item may be tried in magistrates court;

(2) for a second offense, by a fine of not less than two thousand one hundred dollars nor more than five thousand one hundred dollars, and imprisonment for not less than five days nor more than one year. However, the fine imposed by this item must not be suspended in an amount less than one thousand one hundred dollars. If the person's alcohol concentration is at least ten one-hundredths of one percent but less than sixteen one-hundredths of one percent, then the person must be punished by a fine of not less than two thousand five hundred dollars nor more than five thousand five hundred dollars and imprisonment for not less than thirty days nor more than two years. However, the fine imposed by this item must not be suspended in an amount less than one thousand one hundred dollars. If the person's alcohol concentration is sixteen one-hundredths of one percent or more, then the person must be punished by a fine of not less than three thousand five hundred dollars nor more than six thousand five hundred dollars and imprisonment for not less than ninety days nor more than three years. However, the fine imposed by this item must not be suspended in an amount less than one thousand one hundred dollars;

(3) for a third offense, by a fine of not less than three thousand eight

144

hundred dollars nor more than six thousand three hundred dollars, and imprisonment for not less than sixty days nor more than three years. If the person's alcohol concentration is at least ten one-hundredths of one percent but less than sixteen one-hundredths of one percent, then the person must be punished by a fine of not less than five thousand dollars nor more than seven thousand five hundred dollars and imprisonment for not less than ninety days nor more than four years. If the person's alcohol concentration is sixteen one-hundredths of one percent or more, then the person must be punished by a fine of not less than seven thousand five hundred dollars nor more than ten thousand dollars and imprisonment for not less than six months nor more than five years; or

(4) for a fourth or subsequent offense, by imprisonment for not less than one year nor more than five years. If the person's alcohol concentration is at least ten one-hundredths of one percent but less than sixteen one-hundredths of one percent, then the person must be punished by imprisonment for not less than two years nor more than six years. If the person's alcohol concentration is sixteen one-hundredths of one percent or more, then the person must be punished by imprisonment for not less than three years nor more than seven years.

(B) No part of the minimum sentences provided in this section may be suspended. Instead of public service employment the court may invoke another sentence provided in this section. For a second or subsequent offense of this section, the service of the minimum sentence is mandatory. However, the judge may provide for the sentence to be served upon terms and conditions as he considers proper including, but not limited to, weekend service or nighttime service in any fashion he considers necessary.

(C) The fine for a first offense must not be suspended. The court is prohibited from suspending a monetary fine below that of the next preceding minimum monetary fine.

(D) For the purposes of this chapter a conviction, entry of a plea of guilty or of nolo contendere, or forfeiture of bail for the violation of a law or ordinance of this or another state or a municipality of this or another state that prohibits a person from driving a motor vehicle while under the influence of intoxicating liquor, drugs, or narcotics, including, but not limited to, Section 56-5-2930, or prohibits a person from driving a motor vehicle with an unlawful alcohol concentration, including, but not limited to, this section, constitutes a prior offense of this section. Only those violations which occurred within a period of ten years including and immediately preceding the date of the last violation constitute prior violations within the meaning of this section.

(E) Upon imposition of a sentence of public service, the defendant may apply to the court to be allowed to perform his public service in his county of residence if he has been sentenced to public service in a county where he does not reside.

(F) One hundred dollars of each fine imposed pursuant to this section must be placed by the Comptroller General into a special restricted account to be used by the Department of Public Safety for the Highway Patrol.

(G) Two hundred dollars of the fine imposed pursuant to subsections (A)(3) must be placed by the Comptroller General into a special restricted account to be used by the State Law Enforcement Division to offset the costs of administration of the breath testing devices, breath testing site video program, and toxicology laboratory.

(H) A person convicted of violating this section, whether for a first offense or subsequent offense, must enroll in and successfully complete an Alcohol and Drug Safety Action Program certified by the Department of Alcohol and Other Drug Abuse Services. An assessment of the extent and nature of the alcohol and drug abuse problem of the applicant must be prepared and a plan of education or treatment, or both, must be developed for the applicant. The Alcohol and Drug Safety Action Program shall determine if the applicant successfully has completed the services. The applicant must attend the first Alcohol and Drug Safety Action Program available after the date of enrollment. The Department of Alcohol and Other Drug Abuse Services shall determine the cost of services provided by each certified Alcohol and Drug Safety Action Program. Each applicant shall bear the cost of services recommended in the applicant's plan of education or treatment. The cost may not exceed five hundred dollars for education services, two thousand dollars for treatment services, and two thousand five hundred dollars in total for all services. An applicant may not be denied services due to an inability to pay. Inability to pay for services may not be used as a factor in determining if the applicant successfully has completed services. An applicant who is unable to pay for services shall perform fifty hours of community service as arranged by the Alcohol and Drug Safety Action Program, which may use the completion of this community service as a factor in determining if the applicant successfully has completed services. The court must be notified whether an offender failed to enroll in a certified program within thirty days or failed to participate in the plan of education or treatment. The court may hold the individual in contempt of court if the individual cannot show cause as to why no enrollment occurred within the mandated thirty days or why no progress has been made on the plan of education or treatment.

(I) A person charged for a violation of Section 56-5-2930 may be prosecuted pursuant to this section if the original testing of the person's breath or collection of other bodily fluids was performed within two hours of the time of arrest and reasonable suspicion existed to justify the traffic stop. A person may not be prosecuted for both a violation of Section 56-5-2930 and a violation of this section for the same incident. A person who violates the provisions of this section is entitled to a jury trial and is afforded the right to challenge certain factors including the following:

(1) whether or not the person was lawfully arrested or detained;

(2) the period of time between arrest and testing;

(3) whether or not the person was given a written copy of and verbally informed of the rights enumerated in Section 56-5-2950;

147

(4) whether the person consented to taking a test pursuant to Section 56-5-2950, and whether the:

(a) reported alcohol concentration at the time of testing was eight one-hundredths of one percent or more;

(b) individual who administered the test or took samples was qualified pursuant to Section 56-5-2950;

(c) tests administered and samples obtained were conducted pursuant to Section 56-5-2950 and regulations adopted pursuant to Section 56-5-2951(O) and Section 56-5-2953(F); and

(d) machine was working properly.

(J) Nothing contained in this section prohibits the introduction of:

(1) the results of any additional tests of the person's breath or other bodily fluids;

(2) any evidence that may corroborate or question the validity of the breath or bodily fluid test result including, but not limited to:

(a) evidence of field sobriety tests;

(b) evidence of the amount of alcohol consumed by the person; and

(c) evidence of the person's driving;

(3) a video recording of the person's conduct at the incident site and breath testing site taken pursuant to Section 56-5-2953 which is subject to redaction under the South Carolina Rules of Evidence; or

(4) any other evidence of the state of a person's faculties to drive which would call into question the results of a breath or bodily fluid test.

At trial, a person charged with a violation of this section is allowed to present evidence relating to the factors enumerated above and the totality of the evidence produced at trial may be used by the jury to determine guilt or innocence. A person charged with a violation of this section must be given notice of intent to prosecute under the provisions of this section at least thirty calendar days before his trial date.

(K) For the purpose of this section, any offense carrying a penalty of imprisonment of ninety days or less may be tried in magistrates court.

(L) In cases in which enhanced penalties for higher levels of alcohol concentration may be applicable, upon the determination of guilt, the finder of fact shall determine the alcohol concentration and the judge shall apply the appropriate penalty.

**SECTION 56-5-2934. Compulsory process to obtain witnesses and documents; breath testing software.**

Notwithstanding any other provision of law, a person charged with a violation of Section 56-5-2930, 56-5-2933, or 56-5-2945 who is being tried in any court of competent jurisdiction in this State has the right to compulsory process for obtaining witnesses, documents, or both, including, but not limited to, state employees charged with the maintenance of breath testing devices in this State and the administration of breath testing pursuant to this article. This process may be issued under the official signature of the magistrate, judge, clerk, or other officer of the court of competent jurisdiction. The term "documents" includes, but is not limited to, a copy of the computer software program of breath testing devices. SLED must produce all breath testing software in a manner that complies with any and all licensing agreements. This section does not limit a person's ability to obtain breath testing software directly from the manufacturer or distributor.

## SECTION 56-5-2935. Right to jury trial.

Notwithstanding any other provision of law, a person charged with a violation of Section 56-5-2930, 56-5-2933, or 56-5-2945 who is being tried in any court of competent jurisdiction in this State must have the right of trial by jury. A person charged with one or more of these offenses shall enjoy the right to a speedy and public trial by an impartial jury, to be fully informed of the nature and cause of the accusation, to be confronted with the witnesses against him, to have compulsory process for obtaining witnesses, documents, or both, and the right to be fully heard in his defense by himself or by his counsel or, by both.

## SECTION 56-5-2936. Implementation of compulsory testimony requirement postponed; training of employees.

Notwithstanding any other provision of law, the State Law Enforcement Division is not required to implement the provisions of Section 56-5-2934 as contained in Section 9 of Act 390 of 2000 pertaining to the compulsory process for obtaining witnesses including, but not limited to, state employees charged with the maintenance of breath testing devices in this State and the administration of breath testing pursuant to Chapter 5 of Title 56 of the 1976 Code, until the time the General Assembly is adequately able to fund the program or by December 31, 2002, whichever first occurs. Provided, however, by December 31, 2002, the State Law Enforcement Division must have at least three state employees trained and prepared for the purpose of appearing in court and testifying on the maintenance of breath testing devices and the administration of breath testing pursuant to Chapter 5, Title 56 of the 1976 Code.

## SECTION 56-5-2941. Ignition interlock device.

Text of (A) effective until November 19, 2018.

(A) The Department of Motor Vehicles shall require a person who is a resident of this State and who is convicted of violating the provisions of Section 56-5-2930, 56-5-2933, 56-5-2945, 56-5-2947 except if the conviction was for Section 56-5-750, or a law of another state that prohibits a person from driving a motor vehicle while under the influence of alcohol or other drugs, to have installed on any motor vehicle the person drives an ignition interlock device designed to prevent driving of the motor vehicle if the person has consumed alcoholic beverages. This section does not apply to a person convicted of a first offense violation of Section 56-5-2930 or 56-5-2933, unless the person submitted to a breath test pursuant to Section 56-5-2950 and had an alcohol concentration of fifteen one-hundredths of one percent or more. The department may waive the requirements of this section if the department determines that the person has a medical condition that makes the person incapable of properly operating the installed device. If the department grants a medical waiver, the department shall suspend the person's driver's license for the length of time that the person would have been required to hold an ignition interlock restricted license. The department may withdraw the waiver at any time that the department becomes aware that the person's medical condition has improved to the extent that the person has become capable of properly operating an installed device. The department also shall require a person who has enrolled in the Ignition Interlock Device Program in lieu of the remainder of a driver's license suspension or denial of the issuance of a driver's license or permit to have an ignition interlock device installed on any motor vehicle the person drives.

The length of time that a device is required to be affixed to a motor vehicle as set forth in Sections 56-1-286, 56-5-2945, 56-5-2947 except if the conviction was for Sections 56-5-750, 56-5-2951, and 56-5-2990.

Text of (A) effective November 19, 2018.

(A) The Department of Motor Vehicles shall require a person who is a resident of this State and who is convicted of violating the provisions of Sections 56-5-2930, 56-5-2933, 56-5-2945, 56-5-2947 except if the conviction was for Section 56-5-750, or a law of another state that prohibits a person from driving a motor vehicle while under the influence of alcohol or other drugs, to have installed on any motor vehicle the person drives, except a moped, an ignition interlock device designed to prevent driving of the motor vehicle if the person has consumed alcoholic beverages. This section does not apply to a person convicted of a first offense violation of Section 56-5-2930 or 56-5-2933, unless the person submitted to a breath test pursuant to Section 56-5-2950 and had an alcohol concentration of fifteen one-hundredths of one percent or more. The department may waive the requirements of this section if the department determines that the person has a medical condition that makes the person incapable of properly operating the installed device. If the department grants a medical waiver, the department shall suspend the person's driver's license for the length of time that the person would have been required to hold an ignition interlock restricted license. The department may withdraw the waiver at any time that the department becomes aware that the person's medical condition has improved to the extent that the person has become capable of properly operating an installed device. The department also shall require a person who has enrolled in the Ignition Interlock Device Program in lieu of the remainder of a driver's license suspension or denial of the issuance of a driver's license or permit to have an ignition interlock device installed on any motor vehicle the person drives, except a moped.

The length of time that a device is required to be affixed to a motor vehicle as set forth in Sections 56-1-286, 56-5-2945, 56-5-2947 except if the conviction was for Sections 56-5-750, 56-5-2951, and 56-5-2990.

(B) Notwithstanding the pleadings, for purposes of a second or a subsequent offense, the specified length of time that a device is required to be affixed to a motor vehicle is based on the Department of Motor Vehicle's records for offenses pursuant to Section 56-1-286, 56-5-2930, 56-5-2933, 56-5-2945, 56-5-2947 except if the conviction was for Section 56-5-750, 56-5-2950, or 56-5-2951.

(C) If a resident of this State is convicted of violating a law of another state that prohibits a person from driving a motor vehicle while under the influence of alcohol or other drugs, and, as a result of the conviction, the person is subject to an ignition interlock device requirement in the other state, the person is subject to the requirements of this section for the length of time that would have been required for an offense committed in South Carolina, or for the length of time that is required by the other state, whichever is longer.

(D) If a person from another state becomes a resident of South Carolina while subject to an ignition interlock device requirement in another state, the person only may obtain a South Carolina driver's license if the person enrolls in the South Carolina Ignition Interlock Device Program pursuant to this section. The person is subject to the requirements of this section for the length of time that would have been required for an offense committed in South Carolina, or for the length of time that is required by the other state, whichever is longer.

(E) The person must be subject to an Ignition Interlock Device Point System managed by the Department of Probation, Parole and Pardon Services. A person accumulating a total of:

(1) two points or more, but less than three points, must have the length of time that the device is required extended by two months;

(2) three points or more, but less than four points, must have the length of time that the device is required extended by four months, shall submit to a substance abuse assessment pursuant to Section 56-5-2990, and shall successfully complete the plan of education and treatment, or both, as recommended by the certified substance abuse program. Should the person not complete the recommended plan, or not make progress toward completing the plan, the Department of Motor Vehicles shall suspend the person's ignition interlock restricted

license until the plan is completed or progress is being made toward completing the plan;

(3) four points or more must have the person's ignition interlock restricted license suspended for a period of six months, shall submit to a substance abuse assessment pursuant to Section 56-5-2990, and successfully shall complete the plan of education and treatment, or both, as recommended by the certified substance abuse program. Should the person not complete the recommended plan or not make progress toward completing the plan, the Department of Motor Vehicles shall leave the person's ignition interlock restricted license in suspended status, or, if the license has already been reinstated following the six-month suspension, shall resuspend the person's ignition interlock restricted license until the plan is completed or progress is being made toward completing the plan. The Department of Alcohol and Other Drug Abuse Services is responsible for notifying the Department of Motor Vehicles of a person's completion and compliance with education and treatment programs. Upon reinstatement of driving privileges following the six-month suspension, the Department of Probation, Parole and Pardon Services shall reset the person's point total to zero points, and the person shall complete the remaining period of time on the ignition interlock device.

(F) The cost of the device must be borne by the person. However, if the person is indigent and cannot afford the cost of the device, the person may submit an affidavit of indigency to the Department of Probation, Parole and Pardon Services for a determination of indigency as it pertains to the cost of the device. The affidavit of indigency form must be made publicly accessible on the Department of Probation, Parole and Pardon Services' Internet website. If the Department of Probation, Parole and Pardon Services determines that the person is indigent as it pertains to the device, the Department of Probation, Parole and Pardon Services may authorize a device to be affixed to the motor vehicle and the cost of the initial installation and standard use of the device to be paid for by the Ignition Interlock Device Fund managed by the Department of Probation, Parole and

Pardon Services. Funds remitted to the Department of Probation, Parole and Pardon Services for the Ignition Interlock Device Fund also may be used by the Department of Probation, Parole and Pardon Services to support the Ignition Interlock Device Program. For purposes of this section, a person is indigent if the person is financially unable to afford the cost of the ignition interlock device. In making a determination whether a person is indigent, all factors concerning the person's financial conditions should be considered including, but not limited to, income, debts, assets, number of dependents claimed for tax purposes, living expenses, and family situation. A presumption that the person is indigent is created if the person's net family income is less than or equal to the poverty guidelines established and revised annually by the United States Department of Health and Human Services published in the Federal Register. "Net income" means gross income minus deductions required by law. The determination of indigency is subject to periodic review at the discretion of the Department of Probation, Parole and Pardon Services.

(G) The ignition interlock service provider shall collect and remit monthly to the Ignition Interlock Device Fund a fee as determined by the Department of Probation, Parole and Pardon Services not to exceed thirty dollars per month for each month the person is required to drive a vehicle with a device. A service provider who fails to properly remit funds to the Ignition Interlock Device Fund may be decertified as a service provider by the Department of Probation, Parole and Pardon Services. If a service provider is decertified for failing to remit funds to the Ignition Interlock Device Fund, the cost for removal and replacement of a device must be borne by the service provider.

(H)(1) The person shall have the device inspected every sixty days to verify that the device is affixed to the motor vehicle and properly operating, and to allow for the preparation of an ignition interlock device inspection report by the service provider indicating the person's alcohol content at each attempt to start and running retest during each sixty-day period. Failure of the person to have the interlock device

155

inspected every sixty days must result in one ignition interlock device point.

(2) Only a service provider authorized by the Department of Probation, Parole and Pardon Services to perform inspections on ignition interlock devices may conduct inspections. The service provider immediately shall report devices that fail inspection to the Department of Probation, Parole and Pardon Services. The report must contain the person's name, identify the vehicle upon which the failed device is installed, and the reason for the failed inspection.

(3) If the inspection report reflects that the person has failed to complete a running retest, the person must be assessed one ignition interlock device point.

(4) If any inspection report or any photographic images collected by the device shows that the person has violated subsection (M), (O), or (P), the person must be assessed one and one-half ignition interlock device points.

(5) The inspection report must indicate the person's alcohol content at each attempt to start and running retest during each sixty-day period. If the report reflects that the person violated a running retest by having an alcohol concentration of:

(a) two one-hundredths of one percent or more but less than four one-hundredths of one percent, the person must be assessed one-half ignition interlock device point;

(b) four one-hundredths of one percent or more but less than fifteen one-hundredths of one percent, the person must be assessed one ignition interlock device point; or

(c) fifteen one-hundredths of one percent or more, the person must be assessed two ignition interlock device points.

(6) A person may appeal less than four ignition interlock device points

received to an administrative hearing officer with the Department of Probation, Parole and Pardon Services through a process established by the Department of Probation, Parole and Pardon Services. The administrative hearing officer's decision on appeal is final and no appeal from such decision is allowed.

(I)(1) If a person's license is suspended due to the accumulation of four or more ignition interlock device points, the Department of Probation, Parole and Pardon Services must provide a notice of assessment of ignition interlock points which must advise the person of his right to request a contested case hearing before the Office of Motor Vehicle Hearings. The notice of assessment of ignition interlock points also must advise the person that, if he does not request a contested case hearing within thirty days of the issuance of the notice of assessment of ignition interlock points, he waives his right to the administrative hearing and the person's driver's license is suspended pursuant to subsection (E).

(2) The person may seek relief from the Department of Probation, Parole and Pardon Services' determination that a person's license is suspended due to the accumulation of four or more ignition interlock device points by filing a request for a contested case hearing with the Office of Motor Vehicle Hearings pursuant to the Administrative Procedures Act. The filing of the request for a contested case hearing will stay the driver's license suspension pending the outcome of the hearing. However, the filing of the request for a contested case hearing will not stay the requirements of the person having the ignition interlock device.

(3) At the contested case hearing:

(a) the assessment of driver's license suspension can be upheld;

(b) the driver's license suspension can be overturned, or any or all of the contested ignition interlock points included in the device inspection report that results in the contested suspension can be overturned, and the penalties as specified pursuant to subsection (E)

157

will then be imposed accordingly.

(4) A contested case hearing must be held after the request for the hearing is received by the Office of Motor Vehicle Hearings. Nothing in this section prohibits the introduction of evidence at the contested case hearing on the issue of the accuracy of the ignition interlock device. However, if the ignition interlock device is found to not be in working order due to failure of regular maintenance and upkeep by the person challenging the accumulation of ignition interlock points pursuant to the requirement of the ignition interlock program, such allegation cannot serve as a basis to overturn point accumulations.

(5) A written order must be issued by the Office of Motor Vehicle Hearings to all parties either reversing or upholding the assessment of ignition interlock points.

(6) A contested case hearing is governed by the Administrative Procedures Act, and a person has a right to appeal the decision of the hearing officer pursuant to that act to the Administrative Law Court in accordance with its appellate rules. The filing of an appeal does not stay the ignition interlock requirement.

(J) Five years from the date of the person's driver's license reinstatement and every five years thereafter, a fourth or subsequent offender whose license has been reinstated pursuant to Section 56-1-385 may apply to the Department of Probation, Parole and Pardon Services for removal of the ignition interlock device and the removal of the restriction from the person's driver's license. The Department of Probation, Parole and Pardon Services may, for good cause shown, notify the Department of Motor Vehicles that the person is eligible to have the restriction removed from the person's license.

(K)(1) Except as otherwise provided in this section, it is unlawful for a person who is subject to the provisions of this section to drive a motor vehicle that is not equipped with a properly operating, certified ignition interlock device. A person who violates this subsection:

(a) for a first offense, is guilty of a misdemeanor, and, upon conviction, must be fined not less than one thousand dollars or imprisoned not more than one year. The person must have the length of time that the ignition interlock device is required extended by six months;

(b) for a second offense, is guilty of a misdemeanor, and, upon conviction, must be fined not less than five thousand dollars or imprisoned not more than three years. The person must have the length of time that the ignition interlock device is required extended by one year; and

(c) for a third or subsequent offense, is guilty of a felony, and, upon conviction, must be fined not less than ten thousand dollars or imprisoned not more than ten years. The person must have the length of time that the ignition interlock device is required extended by three years.

(2) No portion of the minimum sentence imposed pursuant to this subsection may be suspended.

(3) Notwithstanding any other provision of law, a first or second offense punishable pursuant to this subsection may be tried in summary court.

(L)(1) A person who is required in the course and scope of the person's employment to drive a motor vehicle owned by the person's employer may drive the employer's motor vehicle without installation of an ignition interlock device, provided that the person's use of the employer's motor vehicle is solely for the employer's business purposes.

(2) This subsection does not apply to:

(a) a person convicted of a second or subsequent violation of Section 56-5-2930, 56-5-2933, 56-5-2945, or a law of another state that prohibits a person from driving a motor vehicle while under the influence of alcohol or other drugs, unless the person's driving privileges have been suspended for not less than one year or the person has had an ignition interlock device installed for not less than one year on each of the motor vehicles owned or operated, or both, by the person.

(b) a person who is self employed or to a person who is employed by a business owned in whole or in part by the person or a member of the person's household or immediate family unless during the defense of a criminal charge, the court finds that the vehicle's ownership by the business serves a legitimate business purpose and that titling and registration of the vehicle by the business was not done to circumvent the intent of this section.

(3) Whenever the person operates the employer's vehicle pursuant to this subsection, the person shall have with the person a copy of the Department of Motor Vehicles' form specified by Section 56-1-400(B).

(4) This subsection will be construed in parallel with the requirements of Section 56-1-400(B). A waiver issued pursuant to this subsection will be subject to the same review and revocation as described in Section 56-1-400(B).

(M) It is unlawful for a person to tamper with or disable, or attempt to tamper with or disable, an ignition interlock device installed on a motor vehicle pursuant to this section. Obstructing or obscuring the camera lens of an ignition interlock device constitutes tampering. A person who violates this subsection is guilty of a misdemeanor and, upon conviction, must be fined not more than five hundred dollars or imprisoned not more than thirty days, or both.

(N) It is unlawful for a person to knowingly rent, lease, or otherwise provide a person who is subject to this section with a motor vehicle without a properly operating, certified ignition interlock device. This subsection does not apply if the person began the lease contract period for the motor vehicle prior to the person's arrest for a first offense

160

violation of Section 56-5-2930 or 56-5-2933. A person who violates this subsection is guilty of a misdemeanor, and, upon conviction, must be fined not more than five hundred dollars or imprisoned not more than thirty days, or both.

(O) It is unlawful for a person who is subject to the provisions of this section to solicit or request another person, or for a person to solicit or request another person on behalf of a person who is subject to the provisions of this section, to engage an ignition interlock device to start a motor vehicle with a device installed pursuant to this section or to conduct a running retest while the vehicle is in operation. A person who violates this subsection is guilty of a misdemeanor, and, upon conviction, must be fined not more than five hundred dollars or imprisoned not more than thirty days, or both.

(P) It is unlawful for another person on behalf of a person subject to the provisions of this section to engage an ignition interlock device to start a motor vehicle with a device installed pursuant to this section or to conduct a running retest while that vehicle is in operation. A person who violates this subsection is guilty of a misdemeanor, and, upon conviction, must be fined not more than five hundred dollars or imprisoned not more than thirty days, or both.

(Q) Only ignition interlock devices certified by the Department of Probation, Parole and Pardon Services may be used to fulfill the requirements of this section.

(1) The Department of Probation, Parole and Pardon Services shall certify whether a device meets the accuracy requirements and specifications provided in guidelines or regulations adopted by the National Highway Traffic Safety Administration, as amended from time to time. All devices certified to be used in South Carolina must be set to prohibit the starting of a motor vehicle when an alcohol concentration of two one-hundredths of one percent or more is measured and all running retests must record violations of an alcohol concentration of two one-hundredths of one percent or more, and must capture a photographic image of the driver as the driver is operating

the ignition interlock device. The photographic images recorded by the ignition interlock device may be used by the Department of Probation, Parole and Pardon Services to aid in the Department of Probation, Parole and Pardon Services' management of the Ignition Interlock Device Program; however, neither the Department of Probation, Parole and Pardon Services, the Department of Probation, Parole and Pardon Services' employees, nor any other political subdivision of this State may be held liable for any injury caused by a driver or other person who operates a motor vehicle after the use or attempted use of an ignition interlock device.

(2) The Department of Probation, Parole and Pardon Services shall maintain a current list of certified ignition interlock devices and manufacturers. The list must be updated at least quarterly. If a particular certified device fails to continue to meet federal requirements, the device must be decertified, may not be used until it is compliant with federal requirements, and must be replaced with a device that meets federal requirements. The cost for removal and replacement must be borne by the manufacturer of the noncertified device.

(3) Only ignition interlock installers certified by the Department of Probation, Parole and Pardon Services may install and service ignition interlock devices required pursuant to this section. The Department of Probation, Parole and Pardon Services shall maintain a current list of vendors that are certified to install the devices.

(R) In addition to availability under the Freedom of Information Act, any Department of Probation, Parole and Pardon Services policy concerning ignition interlock devices must be made publicly accessible on the Department of Probation, Parole and Pardon Services' Internet website. Information obtained by the Department of Probation, Parole and Pardon Services and ignition interlock service providers regarding a person's participation in the Ignition Interlock Device Program is to be used for internal purposes only and is not subject to the Freedom of Information Act. A person participating in the Ignition Interlock Device Program or the person's family member may request that the Department of Probation, Parole and Pardon Services provide the person or family member with information obtained by the department and ignition interlock service providers. The Department of Probation, Parole and Pardon Services may release the information to the person or family member at the department's discretion. The Department of Probation, Parole and Pardon Services and ignition interlock service providers must purge all photographic images collected by the device no later than twelve months from the date of the person's completion of the Ignition Interlock Device Program. The Department of Probation, Parole and Pardon Services may retain the images past twelve months if there are any pending appeals or contested case hearings involved with that person, and at their conclusion must purge the images. The Department of Probation, Parole and Pardon Services and ignition interlock service providers must purge all personal information regarding a person's participation in the Ignition Interlock Device Program no later than twelve months from the date of the person's completion of the Ignition Interlock Device Program except for that information which is relevant for pending legal matters.

(S) The Department of Probation, Parole and Pardon Services shall develop policies including, but not limited to, the certification, use, maintenance, and operation of ignition interlock devices and the Ignition Interlock Device Fund.

(T) This section shall apply retroactively to any person currently serving a suspension or denial of the issuance of a license or permit due to a suspension listed in subsection (A).

**SECTION 56-5-2942. Vehicle immobilization after conviction for subsequent violation of Sections 56-5-2930, 56-5-2933, or 56-5-2945; immobilized defined; identity of immobilized vehicle; surrendering of license plates and registration; release of vehicle; hearing; penalties; fees.**

(A) A person who is convicted of or pleads guilty or nolo contendere to a second or subsequent violation of Section 56-5-2930, 56-5-2933, or 56-5-2945 must have all motor vehicles owned by or registered to the person immobilized if the person is a resident of this State, unless the vehicle has been confiscated pursuant to Section 56-5-6240 or the person is a holder of a valid ignition interlock restricted license.

(B) For purposes of this section, "immobilized" and "immobilization" mean suspension and surrender of the registration and motor vehicle license plate.

(C) Upon receipt of a conviction by the department from the court for a second or subsequent violation of Section 56-5-2930, 56-5-2933, or 56-5-2945, the department shall determine all vehicles registered to the person, both solely and jointly, and suspend all vehicles registered to the person, unless the person is a holder of a valid ignition interlock restricted license.

(D) Upon notification by a court in this State or another state of a conviction for a second or subsequent violation of Section 56-5-2930, 56-5-2933, or 56-5-2945, the department shall require the person, unless the person is a holder of a valid ignition interlock restricted license, to surrender all license plates and vehicle registrations subject to immobilization pursuant to this section. The immobilization is for a period of thirty days to take place during the driver's license suspension pursuant to a conviction for a second or subsequent violation of Section 56-5-2930, 56-5-2933, or 56-5-2945. The department shall maintain a record of all vehicles immobilized pursuant to this section.

(E) An immobilized motor vehicle must be released to the holder of a bona fide lien on the motor vehicle when possession of the motor vehicle is requested, as provided by law, by the lienholder for the purpose of foreclosing on and satisfying the lien.

(F) An immobilized motor vehicle may be released by the department without legal or physical restraints to a person who has not been convicted of a second or subsequent violation of Section 56-5-2930, 56-5-2933, or 56-5-2945, if that person is a registered owner of the motor vehicle or a member of the household of a registered owner. The vehicle must be released if an affidavit is submitted by that person to the department stating that:

(1) the person regularly drives the motor vehicle subject to immobilization;

(2) the immobilized motor vehicle is necessary to the person's employment, transportation to an educational facility, or for the performance of essential household duties;

(3) no other motor vehicle is available for the person's use;

(4) the person will not authorize the use of the motor vehicle by any other person known by the person to have been convicted of a second or subsequent violation of Section 56-5-2930, 56-5-2933, or 56-5-2945; or

(5) the person will report immediately to a local law enforcement agency any unauthorized use of the motor vehicle by a person known by the person to have been convicted of a second or subsequent violation of Section 56-5-2930, 56-5-2933, or 56-5-2945.

(G) The department may issue a determination permitting or denying the release of the vehicle based on the affidavit submitted pursuant to subsection (F). A person may seek relief from a department determination immobilizing a motor vehicle or denying the release of the motor vehicle by filing a request for a contested case hearing with the Office of Motor Vehicle Hearings pursuant to the Administrative Procedures Act and the rules of procedure for the Office of Motor Vehicle Hearings.

(H) A person who drives an immobilized motor vehicle except as provided in subsections (E) and (F) is guilty of a misdemeanor, and, upon conviction, must be fined not more than five hundred dollars or imprisoned not more than thirty days.

(I) A person who fails to surrender registrations and license plates pursuant to this section is guilty of a misdemeanor, and, upon conviction, must be fined not more than five hundred dollars or imprisoned not more than thirty days.

(J) A fee of fifty dollars must be paid to the department for each motor vehicle that was suspended before any of the suspended registrations and license plates may be registered or before the motor vehicle may be released pursuant to subsection (F). This fee must be placed by the Comptroller General into the State Highway Fund as established by Section 57-11-20, to be distributed as provided in Section 11-43-167.

(K) For purposes of this article, a conviction of or plea of nolo contendere to Section 56-5-2933 is considered a prior offense of Section 56-5-2930.

### SECTION 56-5-2945. Offense of felony driving under the influence; penalties; "great bodily injury" defined.

(A) A person who, while under the influence of alcohol, drugs, or the combination of alcohol and drugs, drives a motor vehicle and when driving a motor vehicle does any act forbidden by law or neglects any duty imposed by law in the driving of the motor vehicle, which act or neglect proximately causes great bodily injury or death to another person, is guilty of the offense of felony driving under the influence, and, upon conviction, must be punished:

(1) by a mandatory fine of not less than five thousand one hundred dollars nor more than ten thousand one hundred dollars and mandatory imprisonment for not less than thirty days nor more than fifteen years when great bodily injury results;

(2) by a mandatory fine of not less than ten thousand one hundred dollars nor more than twenty-five thousand one hundred dollars and

166

mandatory imprisonment for not less than one year nor more than twenty-five years when death results.

A part of the mandatory sentences required to be imposed by this section must not be suspended, and probation must not be granted for any portion.

(B) As used in this section, "great bodily injury" means bodily injury which creates a substantial risk of death or which causes serious, permanent disfigurement, or protracted loss or impairment of the function of any bodily member or organ.

(C)(1) The Department of Motor Vehicles shall suspend the driver's license of a person who is convicted pursuant to this section. For suspension purposes of this section, convictions arising out of a single incident must run concurrently.

(2) After the person is released from prison, the person shall enroll in the Ignition Interlock Device Program pursuant to Section 56-5-2941, end the suspension, and obtain an ignition interlock restricted license pursuant to Section 56-1-400. The ignition interlock device is required to be affixed to the motor vehicle for three years when great bodily injury results and five years when a death occurs.

(D) One hundred dollars of each fine imposed pursuant to this section must be placed by the Comptroller General into a special restricted account to be used by the Department of Public Safety for the Highway Patrol.

**SECTION 56-5-2946. Submission to testing for alcohol or drugs.**

(A) Notwithstanding any other provision of law, a person must submit to either one or a combination of chemical tests of his breath, blood, or urine for the purpose of determining the presence of alcohol, drugs, or a combination of alcohol and drugs if there is probable cause to believe that the person violated or is under arrest for a violation of Section 56-5-2945.

(B) The tests must be administered at the direction of a law enforcement officer. The administration of one test does not preclude the administration of other tests. The resistance, obstruction, or opposition to testing pursuant to this section is evidence admissible at the trial of the offense which precipitated the requirement for testing. A person who is tested or gives samples for testing may have a qualified person of his choice conduct additional tests at his expense and must be notified of that right. A person's request or failure to request additional blood or urine tests is not admissible against the person in the criminal trial.

(C) The provisions of Section 56-5-2950, relating to the administration of tests to determine a person's alcohol concentration, additional tests at the person's expense, the availability of other evidence on the question of whether or not the person was under the influence of alcohol, drugs, or a combination of them, availability of test information to the person or his attorney, and the liability of medical institutions and persons administering the tests are applicable to this section and also extend to the officer requesting the test, the State or its political subdivisions, or governmental agency, or entity which employs the officer making the request, and the agency, institution, or employer, either governmental or private, of persons administering the tests. Notwithstanding any other provision of state law pertaining to confidentiality of hospital records or other medical records, information regarding tests performed pursuant to this section must be released, upon subpoena, to a court, prosecuting attorney, defense attorney, or law enforcement officer in connection with an alleged violation of Section 56-5-2945.

**SECTION 56-5-2947. Child endangerment; definition; penalties; jurisdiction; evidence for taking child into protective custody.**

(A) A person eighteen years of age or older is guilty of child endangerment when:

(1) the person violates:

(a) Section 56-5-750;

(b) Section 56-5-2930;

(c) Section 56-5-2933; or

(d) Section 56-5-2945; and

(2) the person has one or more passengers younger than sixteen years of age in the motor vehicle when the violation occurs.

If more than one passenger younger than sixteen years of age is in the vehicle when a violation occurs, the person may be charged with only one violation of this section.

(B) Upon conviction, the person must be:

(1) fined not more than one-half of the maximum fine allowed for committing the violation in subsection (A)(1), when the person is fined for that offense;

(2) imprisoned not more than one-half of the maximum term of imprisonment allowed for committing the violation listed in subsection (A)(1), when the person is imprisoned for the offense; or

(3) fined and imprisoned as prescribed in items (1) and (2) when the person is fined and imprisoned for the offense.

(C) No portion of the penalty assessed pursuant to subsection (B) may be suspended or revoked and probation may not be awarded.

(D)(1) In addition to imposing the penalties for offenses listed in subsection (A)(1) and the penalties contained in subsection (B), the Department of Motor Vehicles shall suspend the person's driver's license for sixty days upon conviction under subsection (A)(1)(a). Upon conviction under subsection (A)(1)(b) through (d), the Department of Motor Vehicles shall suspend the person's driver's license.

(2) Upon conviction under subsection (A)(1)(b) through (d), the person shall enroll in the Ignition Interlock Device Program pursuant to Section 56-5-2941, end the suspension, and obtain an ignition interlock restricted license pursuant to Section 56-1-400. The ignition interlock device is required to be affixed to the motor vehicle for three months.

(3) Sections 56-1-1320 and 56-5-2990 as they relate to enrollment in an alcohol and drug safety action program and to the issuance of a provisional driver's license will not be effective until the ignition interlock restricted license period is completed.

(E) A person may be convicted pursuant to this section for child endangerment in addition to being convicted for an offense listed in subsection (A)(1).

(F) The court that has jurisdiction over an offense listed in subsection (A)(1) has jurisdiction over the offense of child endangerment.

(G) A first offense charge for a violation of this section may not be used as the only evidence for taking a child into protective custody pursuant to Sections 63-7-620(A) and 63-7-660.

## SECTION 56-5-2948. Field sobriety tests.

When a person is suspected of causing a motor vehicle incident resulting in the death of another person by the investigating law enforcement officer on the scene of the incident, the driver must submit to field sobriety tests if he is physically able to do so.


## SECTION 56-5-2949. Policies, procedures and regulations on the SLED internet website.

In addition to availability under the Freedom of Information Act, any South Carolina Law Enforcement Division policy, procedure, or regulation concerning breath alcohol testing or breath site video recording which is in effect on or after July 1, 2000, must be made publicly accessible on the SLED Internet web site. A policy, procedure, or regulation may be removed from the SLED web site only after five years from the effective date of the subsequent revision.


## SECTION 56-5-2950. Implied consent to testing for alcohol or drugs; procedures; inference of DUI.

(A) A person who drives a motor vehicle in this State is considered to have given consent to chemical tests of the person's breath, blood, or urine for the purpose of determining the presence of alcohol, drugs, or the combination of alcohol and drugs, if arrested for an offense arising out of acts alleged to have been committed while the person was driving a motor vehicle while under the influence of alcohol, drugs, or a combination of alcohol and drugs. A breath test must be administered at the direction of a law enforcement officer who has arrested a person for driving a motor vehicle in this State while under the influence of alcohol, drugs, or a combination of alcohol and drugs. At the direction of the arresting officer, the person first must be offered a breath test to determine the person's alcohol concentration. If the person is physically unable to provide an acceptable breath sample because the person has an injured mouth, is unconscious or dead, or for any other reason considered acceptable by the licensed medical personnel, the arresting officer may request a blood sample to be taken. If the officer has reasonable suspicion that the person is under the influence of drugs other than alcohol, or is under the influence of a

171

combination of alcohol and drugs, the officer may order that a urine sample be taken for testing. A breath sample taken for testing must be collected within two hours of the arrest. Any additional tests to collect other samples must be collected within three hours of the arrest. The breath test must be administered by a person trained and certified by the South Carolina Criminal Justice Academy, pursuant to SLED policies. Before the breath test is administered, an eight one-hundredths of one percent simulator test must be performed and the result must reflect a reading between 0.076 percent and 0.084 percent. Blood and urine samples must be obtained by physicians licensed by the State Board of Medical Examiners, registered nurses licensed by the State Board of Nursing, and other medical personnel trained to obtain the samples in a licensed medical facility. Blood and urine samples must be obtained and handled in accordance with procedures approved by SLED.

(B) No tests may be administered or samples obtained unless, upon activation of the video recording equipment and prior to the commencement of the testing procedure, the person has been given a written copy of and verbally informed that:

(1) the person does not have to take the test or give the samples, but that the person's privilege to drive must be suspended or denied for at least six months with the option of ending the suspension if the person enrolls in the Ignition Interlock Device Program, if the person refuses to submit to the test, and that the person's refusal may be used against the person in court;

(2) the person's privilege to drive must be suspended for at least one month with the option of ending the suspension if the person enrolls in the Ignition Interlock Device Program, if the person takes the test or gives the samples and has an alcohol concentration of fifteen one-hundredths of one percent or more;

(3) the person has the right to have a qualified person of the person's own choosing conduct additional independent tests at the person's expense;

(4) the person has the right to request a contested case hearing within thirty days of the issuance of the notice of suspension; and

(5) if the person does not request a contested case hearing or if the person's suspension is upheld at the contested case hearing, the person shall enroll in an Alcohol and Drug Safety Action Program.

(C) A hospital, physician, qualified technician, chemist, or registered nurse who obtains the samples or conducts the test or participates in the process of obtaining the samples or conducting the test in accordance with this section is not subject to a cause of action for assault, battery, or another cause alleging that the drawing of blood or taking samples at the request of the arrested person or a law enforcement officer was wrongful. This release from liability does not reduce the standard of medical care required of the person obtaining the samples or conducting the test. This qualified release also applies to the employer of the person who conducts the test or obtains the samples.

(D) The person tested or giving samples for testing may have a qualified person of the person's own choosing conduct additional tests at the person's expense and must be notified in writing of that right. A person's request or failure to request additional blood or urine tests is not admissible against the person in the criminal trial. The failure or inability of the person tested to obtain additional tests does not preclude the admission of evidence relating to the tests or samples obtained at the direction of the law enforcement officer.

(E) The arresting officer shall provide affirmative assistance to the person to contact a qualified person to conduct and obtain additional tests. Affirmative assistance, at a minimum, includes providing transportation for the person to the nearest medical facility which performs blood tests to determine a person's alcohol concentration. If the medical facility obtains the blood sample but refuses or fails to test the blood sample to determine the person's alcohol concentration, SLED shall test the blood sample and provide the result to the person and to the arresting officer. Failure to provide affirmative assistance upon request to obtain additional tests bars the admissibility of the breath test result in a judicial or administrative proceeding.

SLED shall administer the provisions of this subsection and shall make regulations necessary to carry out this subsection's provisions. The costs of the tests administered at the direction of the law enforcement officer must be paid from the state's general fund. However, if the person is subsequently convicted of violating Section 56-5-2930, 56-5-2933, or 56-5-2945, then, upon conviction, the person shall pay twenty-five dollars for the costs of the tests. The twenty-five dollars must be placed by the Comptroller General into a special restricted account to be used by the State Law Enforcement Division to offset the costs of administration of the breath testing devices, breath testing site video program, and toxicology laboratory.

(F) A qualified person who obtains samples or administers the tests or assists in obtaining samples or the administration of tests at the direction of a law enforcement officer is released from civil and criminal liability unless the obtaining of samples or tests is performed in a negligent, reckless, or fraudulent manner. No person may be required by the arresting officer, or by another law enforcement officer, to obtain or take any sample of blood or urine.

(G) In the criminal prosecution for a violation of Section 56-5-2930, 56-5-2933, or 56-5-2945 the alcohol concentration at the time of the test, as shown by chemical analysis of the person's breath or other body fluids, gives rise to the following:

(1) if the alcohol concentration was at that time five one-hundredths of one percent or less, it is conclusively presumed that the person was not under the influence of alcohol;

(2) if the alcohol concentration was at that time in excess of five one-hundredths of one percent but less than eight one-hundredths of one percent, this fact does not give rise to any inference that the person was or was not under the influence of alcohol, but this fact may be

174

considered with other evidence in determining the guilt or innocence of the person; or

(3) if the alcohol concentration was at that time eight one-hundredths of one percent or more, it may be inferred that the person was under the influence of alcohol.

The provisions of this section must not be construed as limiting the introduction of any other evidence bearing upon the question of whether or not the person was under the influence of alcohol, drugs, or a combination of alcohol and drugs.

(H) A person who is unconscious or otherwise in a condition rendering the person incapable of refusal is considered to be informed and not to have withdrawn the consent provided by subsection (A) of this section.

(I) A person required to submit to tests by the arresting law enforcement officer must be provided with a written report including the time of arrest, the time of the tests, and the results of the tests before any trial or other proceeding in which the results of the tests are used as evidence. A person who obtains additional tests shall furnish a copy of the time, method, and results of such tests to the officer before a trial, hearing, or other proceeding in which the person attempts to use the results of the additional tests as evidence.

(J) Policies, procedures, and regulations promulgated by SLED may be reviewed by the trial judge or hearing officer on motion of either party. The failure to follow policies, procedures, and regulations, or the provisions of this section, shall result in the exclusion from evidence of any test results, if the trial judge or hearing officer finds that this failure materially affected the accuracy or reliability of the test results or the fairness of the testing procedure and the court trial judge or hearing officer rules specifically as to the manner in which the failure materially affected the accuracy or reliability of the test results or the fairness of the procedure.

(K) If a state employee charged with the maintenance of breath testing devices in this State and the administration of breath testing policy is required to testify at a contested case hearing or court proceeding, the entity employing the witness may charge a reasonable fee to the defendant for such services.

**SECTION 56-5-2951. Suspension of license for refusal to submit to testing or for certain level of alcohol concentration; temporary alcohol license; administrative hearing; restricted driver's license; penalties.**

(A) The Department of Motor Vehicles shall suspend the driver's license, permit, or nonresident operating privilege of, or deny the issuance of a license or permit to, a person who drives a motor vehicle and refuses to submit to a test provided for in Section 56-5-2950 or has an alcohol concentration of fifteen one-hundredths of one percent or more. The arresting officer shall issue a notice of suspension which is effective beginning on the date of the alleged violation of Section 56-5-2930, 56-5-2933, or 56-5-2945.

(B) Within thirty days of the issuance of the notice of suspension, the person may:

(1) obtain a temporary alcohol license from the Department of Motor Vehicles. A one hundred dollar fee must be assessed for obtaining a temporary alcohol license. Twenty-five dollars of the fee must be distributed by the Department of Motor Vehicles to the Department of Public Safety for supplying and maintaining all necessary vehicle videotaping equipment. The remaining seventy-five dollars must be placed by the Comptroller General into the State Highway Fund as established by Section 57-11-20, to be distributed as provided in Section 11-43-167. The temporary alcohol license allows the person to drive without any restrictive conditions pending the outcome of the contested case hearing provided for in subsection (F) or the final decision or disposition of the matter. If the suspension is upheld at the

contested case hearing, the temporary alcohol license remains in effect until the Office of Motor Vehicle Hearings issues the hearing officer's decision and the Department of Motor Vehicles sends notice to the person that the person is eligible to receive a restricted license pursuant to subsection (H); and

(2) request a contested case hearing before the Office of Motor Vehicle Hearings in accordance with the Office of Motor Vehicle Hearings' rules of procedure.

At the contested case hearing, if:

(a) the suspension is upheld, the person's driver's license, permit, or nonresident operating privilege must be suspended or the person must be denied the issuance of a license or permit for the remainder of the suspension period provided for in subsection (I). Within thirty days of the issuance of the notice that the suspension has been upheld, the person shall enroll in an Alcohol and Drug Safety Action Program pursuant to Section 56-5-2990;

(b) the suspension is overturned, the person must have the person's driver's license, permit, or nonresident operating privilege reinstated.

The provisions of this subsection do not affect the trial for a violation of Section 56-5-2930, 56-5-2933, or 56-5-2945.

(C) The period of suspension provided for in subsection (I) begins on the day the notice of suspension is issued, or at the expiration of any other suspensions, and continues until the person applies for a temporary alcohol license and requests a contested case hearing.

(D) If a person does not request a contested case hearing, the person waives the person's right to the hearing, and the person's suspension must not be stayed but continues for the period provided for in subsection (I).

(E) The notice of suspension must advise the person:

(1) of the person's right to obtain a temporary alcohol driver's license and to request a contested case hearing before the Office of Motor Vehicle Hearings;

(2) the notice of suspension also must advise the person that, if the person does not request a contested case hearing within thirty days of the issuance of the notice of suspension, the person waives the person's right to the contested case hearing, and the suspension continues for the period provided for in subsection (I); and

(3) the notice of suspension also must advise the person that, if the suspension is upheld at the contested case hearing or the person does not request a contested case hearing, the person shall enroll in an Alcohol and Drug Safety Action Program.

(F) A contested case hearing must be held after the request for the hearing is received by the Office of Motor Vehicle Hearings. The scope of the hearing is limited to whether the person:

(1) was lawfully arrested or detained;

(2) was given a written copy of and verbally informed of the rights enumerated in Section 56-5-2950;

(3) refused to submit to a test pursuant to Section 56-5-2950; or

(4) consented to taking a test pursuant to Section 56-5-2950, and the:

(a) reported alcohol concentration at the time of testing was fifteen one-hundredths of one percent or more;

(b) individual who administered the test or took samples was qualified pursuant to Section 56-5-2950;

(c) tests administered and samples obtained were conducted pursuant to Section 56-5-2950; and

178

(d) machine was working properly.

Nothing in this section prohibits the introduction of evidence at the contested case hearing on the issue of the accuracy of the breath test result.

A written order must be issued to all parties either reversing or upholding the suspension of the person's license, permit, or nonresident's operating privilege, or denying the issuance of a license or permit. If the suspension is upheld, the person must receive credit for the number of days the person's license was suspended before the person received a temporary alcohol license and requested the contested case hearing.

The Department of Motor Vehicles and the arresting officer shall have the burden of proof in contested case hearings conducted pursuant to this section. If neither the Department of Motor Vehicles nor the arresting officer appears at the contested case hearing, the hearing officer shall rescind the suspension of the person's license, permit, or nonresident's operating privilege regardless of whether the person requesting the contested case hearing or the person's attorney appears at the contested case hearing.

(G) A contested case hearing is governed by the Administrative Procedures Act, and a person has a right to appeal the decision of the hearing officer pursuant to that act to the Administrative Law Court in accordance with the Administrative Law Court's appellate rules. The filing of an appeal stays the suspension until a final decision is issued on appeal.

(H)(1) If the person did not request a contested case hearing or the suspension is upheld at the contested case hearing, the person shall enroll in an Alcohol and Drug Safety Action Program pursuant to Section 56-5-2990, and may apply for a restricted license if the person is employed or enrolled in a college or university. The restricted license permits the person to drive only to and from work and the person's place of education and in the course of the person's employment or education during the period of suspension. The restricted license also permits the person to drive to and from the Alcohol Drug Safety Action Program classes or to a court-ordered drug program. The department may issue the restricted license only upon showing by the person that the person is employed or enrolled in a college or university, that the person lives further than one mile from the person's place of employment, place of education, or location of the person's Alcohol and Drug Safety Action Program classes, or the location of the person's court-ordered drug program, and that there is no adequate public transportation between the person's residence and the person's place of employment, the person's place of education, the location of the person's Alcohol and Drug Safety Action Program classes, or the location of the person's court-ordered drug program.

(2) If the department issues a restricted license pursuant to this subsection, the department shall designate reasonable restrictions on the times during which and routes on which the person may drive a motor vehicle. A change in the employment hours, place of employment, status as a student, status of attendance of Alcohol and Drug Safety Action Program classes, status of attendance of the person's court-ordered drug program, or residence must be reported immediately to the department by the person.

(3) The fee for a restricted license is one hundred dollars, but no additional fee may be charged because of changes in the place and hours of employment, education, or residence. Twenty dollars of this fee must be deposited in the state's general fund, and eighty dollars must be placed by the Comptroller General into the State Highway Fund as established by Section 57-11-20, to be distributed as provided in Section 11-43-167.

(4) Driving a motor vehicle outside the time limits and route imposed by a restricted license is a violation of Section 56-1-460.

(I)(1) Except as provided in item (3), the period of a driver's license, permit, or nonresident operating privilege suspension for, or denial of issuance of a license or permit to, an arrested person who has no previous convictions for violating Section 56-5-2930, 56-5-2933, or 56-5-2945, or a law of another state that prohibits a person from driving a motor vehicle while under the influence of alcohol or other drugs within the ten years preceding a violation of this section, and who has had no previous suspension imposed pursuant to Section 56-1-286, 56-5-2951, or 56-5-2990, within the ten years preceding a violation of this section is:

(a) six months for a person who refuses to submit to a test pursuant to Section 56-5-2950; or

(b) one month for a person who takes a test pursuant to Section 56-5-2950 and has an alcohol concentration of fifteen one-hundredths of one percent or more.

(2) The period of a driver's license, permit, or nonresident operating privilege suspension for, or denial of issuance of a license or permit to, a person who has been convicted previously for violating Section 56-5-2930, 56-5-2933, or 56-5-2945, or another law of this State or another state that prohibits a person from driving a motor vehicle while under the influence of alcohol or another drug within the ten years preceding a violation of this section, or who has had a previous suspension imposed pursuant to Section 56-1-286, 56-5-2951, or 56-5-2990, within the ten years preceding a violation of this section is:

(a) for a second offense, nine months if the person refuses to submit to a test pursuant to Section 56-5-2950, or two months if the person takes a test pursuant to Section 56-5-2950 and has an alcohol concentration of fifteen one-hundredths of one percent or more;

(b) for a third offense, twelve months if the person refuses to submit to a test pursuant to Section 56-5-2950, or three months if the person takes a test pursuant to Section 56-5-2950 and has an alcohol concentration of fifteen one-hundredths of one percent or more; and

(c) for a fourth or subsequent offense, fifteen months if the person refuses to submit to a test pursuant to Section 56-5-2950, or four months if the person takes a test pursuant to Section 56-5-2950 and has an alcohol concentration of fifteen one-hundredths of one percent or more.

(3) In lieu of serving the remainder of a suspension or denial of the issuance of a license or permit, a person may enroll in the Ignition Interlock Device Program pursuant to Section 56-5-2941, end the suspension or denial of the issuance of a license or permit, and obtain an ignition interlock restricted license pursuant to Section 56-1-400. The ignition interlock device is required to be affixed to the motor vehicle equal to the length of time remaining on the person's suspension or denial of the issuance of a license or permit. If the length of time remaining is less than three months, the ignition interlock device is required to be affixed to the motor vehicle for three months. Once a person has enrolled in the Ignition Interlock Device Program and obtained an ignition interlock restricted license, the person is subject to Section 56-5-2941 and cannot subsequently choose to serve the suspension.

(J) A person's driver's license, permit, or nonresident operating privilege must be restored when the person's period of suspension or ignition interlock restricted license requirement pursuant to subsection (I) has concluded, even if the person has not yet completed the Alcohol and Drug Safety Action Program. After the person's driving privilege is restored, the person shall continue the services of the Alcohol and Drug Safety Action Program. If the person withdraws from or in any way stops making satisfactory progress toward the completion of the Alcohol and Drug Safety Action Program, the person's license must be suspended until the completion of the Alcohol and Drug Safety Action Program. A person shall be attending or have completed an Alcohol and Drug Safety Action Program pursuant to Section 56-5-2990 before the person's driving privilege can be restored at the conclusion of the suspension period or ignition interlock restricted license requirement.

(K) When a nonresident's privilege to drive a motor vehicle in this

State has been suspended pursuant to the provisions of this section, the department shall give written notice of the action taken to the motor vehicle administrator of the state of the person's residence and of any state in which the person has a license or permit.

(L) The department shall not suspend the privilege to drive of a person under the age of twenty-one pursuant to Section 56-1-286, if the person's privilege to drive has been suspended pursuant to this section arising from the same incident.

(M) A person whose driver's license or permit is suspended pursuant to this section is not required to file proof of financial responsibility.

(N) An insurer shall not increase premiums on, add surcharges to, or cancel the automobile insurance of a person charged with a violation of Section 56-1-286, 56-5-2930, 56-5-2933, 56-5-2945, or a law of another state that prohibits a person from driving a motor vehicle while under the influence of alcohol or other drugs based solely on the violation unless the person is convicted of the violation.

(O) The department shall administer the provisions of this section.

(P) If a person does not request a contested case hearing within the thirty-day period as authorized pursuant to this section, the person may file with the department a form after enrolling in a certified Alcohol and Drug Safety Action Program to apply for a restricted license. The restricted license permits him to drive only to and from work and his place of education and in the course of his employment or education during the period of suspension. The restricted license also permits him to drive to and from Alcohol and Drug Safety Action Program classes or a court-ordered drug program. The department may issue the restricted license at any time following the suspension upon a showing by the individual that he is employed or enrolled in a college or university, that he lives further than one mile from his place of employment, place of education, the location of his Alcohol and Drug Safety Action Program classes, or the location of his court-ordered drug program, and that there is no adequate public transportation between his residence and his place of employment, his place of education, the location of his Alcohol and Drug Safety Action Program classes, or the location of his court-ordered drug program. The department must designate reasonable restrictions on the times during which and routes on which the individual may drive a motor vehicle. A change in the employment hours, place of employment, status as a student, status of attendance of Alcohol and Drug Safety Action Program classes, status of his court-ordered drug program, or residence must be reported immediately to the department by the licensee. The route restrictions, requirements, and fees imposed by the department for the issuance of the restricted license issued pursuant to this item are the same as those provided in this section had the person requested a contested case hearing. A restricted license is valid until the person successfully completes a certified Alcohol and Drug Safety Action Program, unless the person fails to complete or make satisfactory progress to complete the program.

## SECTION 56-5-2952. Filing fee to request contested case hearing.

The filing fee to request a contested case hearing before the Office of Motor Vehicle Hearings of the Administrative Law Court is two hundred dollars, or as otherwise prescribed by the rules of procedure for the Office of Motor Vehicle Hearings. Funds generated from the collection of this fee must be retained by the Administrative Law Court, provided, however, that these funds first must be used to meet the expenses of the Office of Motor Vehicle Hearings, including the salaries of its employees, as directed by the chief judge of the Administrative Law Court.

## SECTION 56-5-2953. Incident site and breath test site video recording.

(A) A person who violates Section 56-5-2930, 56-5-2933, or 56-5-

2945 must have his conduct at the incident site and the breath test site video recorded.

(1)(a) The video recording at the incident site must:

(i) not begin later than the activation of the officer's blue lights;

(ii) include any field sobriety tests administered; and

(iii) include the arrest of a person for a violation of Section 56-5-2930 or Section 56-5-2933, or a probable cause determination in that the person violated Section 56-5-2945, and show the person being advised of his Miranda rights.

(b) A refusal to take a field sobriety test does not constitute disobeying a police command.

(2) The video recording at the breath test site must:

(a) include the entire breath test procedure, the person being informed that he is being video recorded, and that he has the right to refuse the test;

(b) include the person taking or refusing the breath test and the actions of the breath test operator while conducting the test; and

(c) also include the person's conduct during the required twenty-minute pre-test waiting period, unless the officer submits a sworn affidavit certifying that it was physically impossible to video record this waiting period.

(3) The video recordings of the incident site and of the breath test site are admissible pursuant to the South Carolina Rules of Evidence in a criminal, administrative, or civil proceeding by any party to the action.

(B) Nothing in this section may be construed as prohibiting the introduction of other relevant evidence in the trial of a violation of

Section 56-5-2930, 56-5-2933, or 56-5-2945. Failure by the arresting officer to produce the video recording required by this section is not alone a ground for dismissal of any charge made pursuant to Section 56-5-2930, 56-5-2933, or 56-5-2945 if the arresting officer submits a sworn affidavit certifying that the video recording equipment at the time of the arrest or probable cause determination, or video equipment at the breath test facility was in an inoperable condition, stating which reasonable efforts have been made to maintain the equipment in an operable condition, and certifying that there was no other operable breath test facility available in the county or, in the alternative, submits a sworn affidavit certifying that it was physically impossible to produce the video recording because the person needed emergency medical treatment, or exigent circumstances existed. In circumstances including, but not limited to, road blocks, traffic accident investigations, and citizens' arrests, where an arrest has been made and the video recording equipment has not been activated by blue lights, the failure by the arresting officer to produce the video recordings required by this section is not alone a ground for dismissal. However, as soon as video recording is practicable in these circumstances, video recording must begin and conform with the provisions of this section. Nothing in this section prohibits the court from considering any other valid reason for the failure to produce the video recording based upon the totality of the circumstances; nor do the provisions of this section prohibit the person from offering evidence relating to the arresting law enforcement officer's failure to produce the video recording.

(C) A video recording must not be disposed of in any manner except for its transfer to a master recording for consolidation purposes until the results of any legal proceeding in which it may be involved are finally determined.

(D) SLED is responsible for purchasing, maintaining, and supplying all necessary video recording equipment for use at the breath test sites. SLED also is responsible for monitoring all breath test sites to ensure the proper maintenance of video recording equipment. The Department of Public Safety is responsible for purchasing, maintaining, and supplying all videotaping equipment for use in all

186

law enforcement vehicles used for traffic enforcement. The Department of Public Safety also is responsible for monitoring all law enforcement vehicles used for traffic enforcement to ensure proper maintenance of video recording equipment.

(E) Beginning one month from the effective date of this section, all of the funds received in accordance with Section 14-1-208(C)(9) must be expended by SLED to equip all breath test sites with video recording devices and supplies. Once all breath test sites have been equipped fully with video recording devices and supplies, eighty-seven and one-half percent of the funds received in accordance with Section 14-1-208(C)(9) must be expended by the Department of Public Safety to purchase, maintain, and supply video recording equipment for vehicles used for traffic enforcement. The remaining twelve and one-half percent of the funds received in accordance with Section 14-1-208(C)(9) must be expended by SLED to purchase, maintain, and supply video recording equipment for the breath test sites. Funds must be distributed by the State Treasurer to the Department of Public Safety and SLED on a monthly basis. The Department of Public Safety and SLED are authorized to carry forward any unexpended funds received in accordance with Section 14-1-208(C)(9) as of June thirtieth of each year and to expend these carried forward funds for the purchase, maintenance, and supply of video recording equipment. The Department of Public Safety and SLED must report the revenue received under this section and the expenditures for which the revenue was used as required in the department's and SLED's annual appropriation request to the General Assembly.

(F) The Department of Public Safety and SLED must promulgate regulations necessary to implement the provisions of this section.

(G) The provisions contained in Section 56-5-2953(A), (B), and (C) take effect for each law enforcement vehicle used for traffic enforcement once the law enforcement vehicle is equipped with a video recording device. The provisions contained in Section 56-5-2953(A), (B), and (C) take effect for a breath test site once the breath test site is equipped with a video recording device.

## SECTION 56-5-2954. Breath testing sites; records of problems with devices.

The State Law Enforcement Division and each law enforcement agency with a breath testing site is required to maintain a detailed record of malfunctions, repairs, complaints, or other problems regarding breath testing devices at each site. These records must be electronically recorded. These records, including any and all remarks, must be entered into a breath testing device and subsequently made available on the State Law Enforcement Division web site. The records required by this section are subject to compulsory process issued by any court of competent jurisdiction in this State and are public records under the Freedom of Information Act.

## SECTION 56-5-2955. Admissibility of evidence obtained under Section 56-5-2950.

Any evidence obtained under the provisions of Section 56-5-2950 shall not be admissible as evidence to prove a criminal offense other than those offenses delineated in Title 56.

## SECTION 56-5-2970. Reports to Department of Motor Vehicle of convictions, certain pleas and bail forfeitures.

All clerks of court, magistrates, city recorders, and other public officers in this State having charge or responsibility with respect to convictions or of the entry of pleas of guilty or of nolo contendere or of the forfeitures of bail posted for violation of Section 56-5-2930, 56-5-2933, or for convictions or of the entry of pleas of guilty or of nolo contendere or of the forfeitures of bail posted for violations of any other laws or ordinances of this State that prohibit any person from operating a motor vehicle while under the influence of intoxicating liquor, drugs, or narcotics are required to report to the Department of Motor Vehicles every such conviction, plea of guilty or of nolo contendere or bail forfeiture within ten days after such conviction, entry of a plea of guilty or of nolo contendere or forfeiture or after the receipt of such report, as the case may be. Such reports shall be made upon forms to be provided by the department, arranged in duplicate, and the director of the Department of Motor Vehicles shall acknowledge the filing of each such report by signing the duplicate of such report and returning it to the officer making it, to be kept by such officer as evidence of his compliance with the requirement that he make such report.

Any person violating the provisions of this section shall be subject to a penalty of twenty-five dollars for each such failure, to be collected by the Attorney General or the solicitors of the State under the direction of the Attorney General and paid into the general fund of the State.

**SECTION 56-5-2980. Copies of reports as prima facie evidence of certain matters; effect of stipulating subsequent offense.**

In all trials and proceedings in any court of this State in which the defendant is charged with a violation of Section 56-5-2920, 56-5-2930, or 56-5-2933, photostatic, optical disk, or other copies of the reports required to be filed with the Department of Motor Vehicles pursuant to Section 56-5-2970 shall be deemed prima facie evidence of the information contained on such reports for the purpose of showing any previous conviction of the defendant in any other court. Copies of the reports must be duly certified by the director of the department or his designee as true copies. If the defendant stipulates that the charge constitutes a second or subsequent offense, the indictment shall not contain allegations of prior offenses and evidence of such prior offenses must not be introduced.

**SECTION 56-5-2990. Suspension of convicted person's driver's license; period of suspension.**

(A)(1) The Department of Motor Vehicles shall suspend the driver's license of a person who is convicted for a violation of Section 56-5-2930, 56-5-2933, or a law of another state that prohibits a person from driving a motor vehicle while under the influence of alcohol or other drugs.

(2) For a first offense:

(a) If a person is found to have refused to submit to a breath test pursuant to Section 56-5-2950 and is convicted of Section 56-5-2930 or 56-5-2933, the person's driver's license must be suspended six months. The person is not eligible for a provisional license pursuant to Article 7, Chapter 1, Title 56. In lieu of serving the remainder of the suspension, the person may enroll in the Ignition Interlock Device Program pursuant to Section 56-5-2941, end the suspension, and obtain an ignition interlock restricted license pursuant to Section 56-1-400. The ignition interlock device is required to be affixed to the motor vehicle equal to the length of time remaining on the person's suspension. If the length of time remaining is less than three months, the ignition interlock device is required to be affixed to the motor vehicle for three months. Once a person has enrolled in the Ignition Interlock Device Program and obtained an ignition interlock restricted license, the person is subject to Section 56-5-2941 and cannot subsequently choose to serve the suspension.

(b) If a person submitted to a breath test pursuant to Section 56-5-2950 and is convicted of having an alcohol concentration of less than fifteen one-hundredths of one percent, the person's driver's license must be suspended six months. The person is eligible for a provisional license pursuant to Article 7, Chapter 1, Title 56. In lieu of serving the remainder of the suspension, the person may enroll in the Ignition Interlock Device Program pursuant to Section 56-5-2941, end the suspension, and obtain an ignition interlock restricted license pursuant to Section 56-1-400. The ignition interlock device is required to be affixed to the motor vehicle equal to the length of time remaining on the person's suspension. If the length of time remaining is less than three months, the ignition interlock device is required to be affixed to the motor vehicle for three months. Once a person has enrolled in the Ignition Interlock Device Program and obtained an ignition interlock restricted license, the person is subject to Section 56-5-2941 and cannot subsequently choose to serve the suspension.

(c) If a person submitted to a breath test pursuant to Section 56-5-2950 and is convicted of having an alcohol concentration of fifteen one-hundredths of one percent or more, the person shall enroll in the Ignition Interlock Device Program pursuant to Section 56-5-2941, end the suspension, and obtain an ignition interlock restricted license pursuant to Section 56-1-400. The ignition interlock device is required to be affixed to the motor vehicle for six months. The person is not eligible for a provisional license pursuant to Article 7, Chapter 1, Title 56.

(3) For a second offense, a person shall enroll in the Ignition Interlock Device Program pursuant to Section 56-5-2941, end the suspension, and obtain an ignition interlock restricted license pursuant to Section 56-1-400. The ignition interlock device is required to be affixed to the motor vehicle for two years.

(4) For a third offense, a person shall enroll in the Ignition Interlock Device Program pursuant to Section 56-5-2941, end the suspension, and obtain an ignition interlock restricted license pursuant to Section 56-1-400. The ignition interlock device is required to be affixed to the motor vehicle for three years. If the third offense occurs within five years from the date of the first offense, the ignition interlock device is required to be affixed to the motor vehicle for four years.

(5) For a fourth or subsequent offense, a person shall enroll in the Ignition Interlock Device Program pursuant to Section 56-5-2941, end the suspension, and obtain an ignition interlock restricted license

pursuant to Section 56-1-400. The ignition interlock device is required to be affixed to the motor vehicle for life.

(6) Except as provided in subsection (A)(4), only those offenses which occurred within ten years, including and immediately preceding the date of the last offense, shall constitute prior offenses within the meaning of this section.

(B) A person whose license is suspended pursuant to this section, Section 56-1-286, 56-5-2945, or 56-5-2951 must be notified by the department of the suspension and of the requirement to enroll in and successfully complete an Alcohol and Drug Safety Action Program certified by the Department of Alcohol and Other Drug Abuse Services. A person who must complete an Alcohol and Drug Safety Action Program as a condition of reinstatement of his driving privileges or a court-ordered drug program may use the route restricted or special restricted driver's license to attend the Alcohol and Drug Safety Action Program classes or court-ordered drug program in addition to the other permitted uses of a route restricted driver's license or a special restricted driver's license. An assessment of the extent and nature of the alcohol and drug abuse problem, if any, of the person must be prepared and a plan of education or treatment, or both, must be developed for the person. Entry into the services, if the services are necessary, recommended in the plan of education or treatment, or both, developed for the person is a mandatory requirement of the issuance of an ignition interlock restricted license to the person whose license is suspended pursuant to this section. Successful completion of the services, if the services are necessary, recommended in the plan of education or treatment, or both, developed for the person is a mandatory requirement of the full restoration of driving privileges to the person whose license is suspended pursuant to this section. The Alcohol and Drug Safety Action Program shall determine if the person has successfully completed the services. Alcohol and Drug Safety Action Programs shall meet at least once a month. The person whose license is suspended shall attend the first Alcohol and Drug Safety Action Program available after the date of enrollment.

(C) The Department of Alcohol and Other Drug Abuse Services shall determine the cost of services provided by each certified Alcohol and Drug Safety Action Program. Each person shall bear the cost of services recommended in the person's plan of education or treatment. The cost may not exceed five hundred dollars for education services, two thousand dollars for treatment services, and two thousand five hundred dollars in total for all services. No person may be denied services due to an inability to pay. Inability to pay for services may not be used as a factor in determining if the person has successfully completed services. A person who is unable to pay for services shall perform fifty hours of community service as arranged by the Alcohol and Drug Safety Action Program, which may use the completion of this community service as a factor in determining if the person has successfully completed services. The Department of Alcohol and Other Drug Abuse Services shall report annually to the House Ways and Means Committee and Senate Finance Committee on the number of first and multiple offenders completing the Alcohol and Drug Safety Action Program, the amount of fees collected and expenses incurred by each Alcohol and Drug Safety Action Program, and the number of community service hours performed in lieu of payment.

(D) If the person has not successfully completed the services as directed by the Alcohol and Drug Safety Action Program within one year of enrollment, a hearing must be provided by the Alcohol and Drug Safety Action Program whose decision is appealable to the Department of Alcohol and Other Drug Abuse Services. If the person is unsuccessful in the Alcohol and Drug Safety Action Program, the Department of Motor Vehicles may waive the successful completion of the program as a mandatory requirement of the issuance of an ignition interlock restricted license upon the recommendation of the Medical Advisory Board as utilized by the Department of Motor Vehicles, if the Medical Advisory Board determines public safety and welfare of the person may not be endangered.

(E) The Department of Motor Vehicles and the Department of Alcohol and Other Drug Abuse Services shall develop procedures necessary for the communication of information pertaining to relicensing, or otherwise. These procedures must be consistent with the confidentiality laws of the State and the United States. If a person's driver's license is suspended pursuant to this section, an insurance company shall not refuse to issue insurance to cover the remaining members of the person's family, but the insurance company is not liable for any actions of the person whose license has been suspended or who has voluntarily turned the person's license in to the Department of Motor Vehicles.

(F) Except as provided for in Section 56-1-365(D) and (E), the driver's license suspension periods under this section begin on the date the person is convicted, receives sentence upon a plea of guilty or of nolo contendere, or forfeits bail posted for the a violation of Section 56-5-2930, 56-5-2933, or for the violation of any other a law of this State or ordinance of a county or municipality of this State that prohibits a person from operating a motor vehicle while under the influence of intoxicating liquor, or narcotics; however, a person is not prohibited from filing a notice of appeal and receiving a certificate which entitles him to operate a motor vehicle for a period of sixty days after the conviction, plea of guilty or nolo contendere, or bail forfeiture pursuant to Section 56-1-365(F).

### SECTION 56-5-2995. Additional assessment on persons convicted of driving under influence of intoxicating liquors or drugs.

(A) In addition to the penalties imposed for a first offense violation of Section 56-5-2930 or 56-5-2933 in magistrate's or municipal court, an additional assessment of twelve dollars must be added to any punishment imposed which must be remitted to the State Treasurer who shall then distribute the twelve-dollar assessments in the manner provided in Section 14-1-201.

(B) In addition to the penalties and assessments imposed for a second or subsequent violation of Section 56-5-2930, 56-5-2933, or a

194

violation of Section 56-5-2945 in general sessions court, an additional assessment of twelve dollars must be added to any punishment imposed which must be remitted to the State Treasurer who shall then distribute these twelve-dollar assessments in the manner provided in Section 14-1-201.

Made in the USA
Columbia, SC
22 February 2021

33341927R00114